COOL AUDITOR

COOL AUDITOR

POEMS BY

RAY GONZALEZ

BOA Editions, Ltd. ❧ Rochester, N.Y. ❧ 2009

First Edition
09 10 11 12 7 6 5 4 3 2 1

For information about permission to reuse any material from this book please contact The Permissions Company at www.permissionscompany.com or e-mail permdude@eclipse.net.

Publications by BOA Editions, Ltd. – a not-for-profit corporation under section 501 (c) (3) of the United States Internal Revenue Code – are made possible with funds from a variety of sources, including public funds from the New York State Council on the Arts, a state agency; the Literature Program of the National Endowment for the Arts; the County of Monroe, NY; the Lannan Foundation for support of the Lannan Translations Selection Series; the Sonia Raiziss Giop Charitable Foundation; the Mary S. Mulligan Charitable Trust; the Rochester Area Community Foundation; the Arts & Cultural Council for Greater Rochester; the Steeple-Jack Fund; the Ames-Amzalak Memorial Trust in memory of Henry Ames, Semon Amzalak and Dan Amzalak; and contributions from many individuals nationwide.

See Colophon on page 104 for special individual acknowledgements.

Cover Design: Sandy Knight
Cover Art: Robert Marx
Interior Design and Composition: Bill Jones
BOA Logo: Mirko

Library of Congress Cataloging-in-Publication Data

Gonzalez, Ray.
Cool auditor : prose poems / by Ray Gonzalez. -- 1st ed.
    p.cm.
ISBN 978-1-934414-29-3 (pbk.)
I. Title

PS3557.O476C663 2009
811'.54--dc22

2008037953

NATIONAL
ENDOWMENT
FOR THE ARTS
A great nation
deserves great art.

BOA Editions, Ltd.
Nora A. Jones, Executive Director/Publisher
Thom Ward, Editor/Production
Peter Conners, Editor/Marketing
Bernadette Catalana, BOA Board Chair
A. Poulin, Jr., Founder (1938-1996)
250 North Goodman Street, Suite 306
Rochester, NY 14607
www.boaeditions.org

State of the Arts
NYSCA

CONTENTS

PART 1

PART 2

PART 3

In memory of Julio Cortázar

PART 1

BEGINNING WITH TWO LINES FROM KENNETH REXROTH

I see the unwritten books, the unrecorded experiments, the unpainted pictures, the interrupted lives, a staircase leading to a guarantee, the glowing frame of wisdom protecting me from harm after I escape the questions of a lifetime. I see the turning of the pages in a book I have not read, its story proclaiming the reader is going to escape without knowing how the equation injured the moment—sacred leaves rotting in a bottle of rubbing oil, their black designs sinking farther than my reach.

I witness what is made for someone else, its motion calling me to wait for the regions of love where we come back, able to dismiss the picture of ourselves where we can't smile because no one is able to capture time that has not happened and never will. There is no agony and waste, only the steps into the frontier where it is easy to hide.

Even a shoulder bone cracks in the morning light, a man rising at the end of a century where everyone gives him pictures, including one of a translucent scene where the running youth carries the host, his confusion between danger and desire making the boy stop at the bank of the river, turn, and go home. When he gets to the house, he doesn't cry out. When it goes dark and the arguments begin, it is his portrait that is handed to me first because I already arrived at the junction between the lamp and the staircase to the mocking stars.

THE SAME WINDOW

What should I say? That Nostradamus uttered in a strange tongue only known to him as he wrote down his prophecies? Perhaps I should mention the theory that peacocks are proud of their beautiful tails and feathers, but the peacock scream comes each time the bird looks down and sees its ugly, black foot. Even my father, writing in a gnomic book, told me that the bandit beheaded in his boyhood village was the man who ran away with my father's grandmother. What does this have to do with Amsterdam, San Francisco, or the brittle streets of El Paso? Where should I sweat next? Someone wrote that Columbus scribbled frantic notes on the margins of a manuscript by Marco Polo. If textbook heroes were part of my schoolboy fantasies, I won first place in a fourth-grade art contest by drawing the Niña, Pinta, and Santa Maria, swallowing my Texas education that said the magic aspect of life had to do with great discovery by three Spanish ships and my brown skin was simply an evolutionary mistake—a hidden conquest of genes and DNA no talented fourth grader could conceive in his wildest crayon colored dreams. Yet, what was the year when I made my first cardboard electric guitar, taping an empty cigar box my father gave me onto a yardstick I stole from my mother, the teacher? The box was the body of the guitar and the ruler was the neck marked with precise frets where I rocked out and did air guitar to early Beatles. What should I sing next because a tune titled "Alligator Elevator" has been ringing in my head for days. I have not invented the lyrics because a dog crossed the street in search of the swimming reptile on the same day I thought of the title. I imagine the secrecy of elevators must be kept from the world because today, as I waited for the first winter snow, I saw beautiful Chinese silk being passed from hand to hand, the shoulders of the traders obscured in the tremendous flakes of white that erased further celebration and put me in a position to praise the details associated with a strange intelligence I found escaping through the window. This made me recall the day Lao-Tse told me he was carried in his mother's body for sixty-two years, and that is why his hair was white at birth.

TEN OBJECTS

Lordosis—inward curvature of the spine
Self-conquest—to overcome one's worst characteristics
Genotype—the genetic constitution of an individual
Belladonna—deadly nightshade

Taking the belladonna affects the genotype, which prevents self-conquest but allows a severe case of lordosis to take place.

Picking the belladonna strains the lordosis and moves some DNA, thus redefining the geonotype without the brain considering self-conquest.

Overcoming the need for self-conquest cancels that day's search for belladonna, instigating a new strain that, once again, shifts the genotype and lessens the pain of lordosis.

The lordosis points the individual toward the earth, making it easier to pick the belladonna without the danger of upsetting the balance between the current genotype and the self-conquest in the background.

The genotype is not necessarily the driving force behind clearing the field of belladonna because the lordosis prevents such a sweeping and creates desire, thus bringing self-conquest back into the picture.

Self-conquest makes the belladonna grow at the borders of vision, moving the individual with the painful lordosis toward newer territory where the genotype has a clearer path to the healing sun.

The belladonna prefers darkness, so the genotype is twisted in an unexpected path that begins to heal the lordosis and leaves self-conquest up in the air.

Lordosis is a path given toward self-conquest when the genotype of belladonna is felt.

Genotypes are stored in the ribs, their invisible evolution forcing self-conquest that avoids lordosis after the consumption of belladonna.

The belladonna in the ground resembles a curved spine.

AVAILABLE FOR AN EPIPHANY

The longest word used by Shakespeare in any of his works is honorificabilitudinitatibus. It doesn't mean the lone black hair that sticks out of your big right toe just below the toenail. The word for that hair is slypadorelystybold. Pregnant goldfish are called twits, but my father used to call me a dummy, a goof-ball like those stinking moth balls in the closet that held his four pair of golf shoes whose spikes dug into the carpet, a detail I remember because my slarapin is alive. In other words, my second heart—that one that resides inside my soul and beats for the past and is able to put these things together. Graffito is the little-used singular of the much used plural word graffiti, but manes is not the plural for more than one moon, because to mistake mane for moon would mean I could not rise in the middle of the night, suffering from insomnia, and write something about a moon I have not seen in months, my words glowing on my computer screen brighter than the graffito I dreamed about when a friend of one of my nephews was gunned down in a drive-by. Narcissism is the psychiatric term for self-love as in the lone artist compelled to ignore his masterpiece leaning on the canvas because the cracked mirror in his tiny apartment is showing him many stark visions he conjures through powerful fumes rising out of the dozens of tubes of oil paints that are squashed all over the floor.

A language becomes extinct in this world every two weeks. A silence fills the halls every three months, its source a secret, its ability to slow the development of rapture a potent thing that is best avoided from dusk to dawn, though one vital moment appears on the border of light and darkness as if something is about to touch those of us who have even the slightest clue as to what is going on. In 1961, Italian-artist Piero Manzoni packed his feces in cans, signed and mounted them, and then sold them as art. This story about the natural elements of man is a common one, an epic no artist or writer is able to comprehend because the canned stuff is the purest form of artistic expression. The fact it is imprisoned in a container is a metaphor about imaginative souls who create anything in order to get from here to there without having to step on too much shit or having to face what their mighty and private visions are truly made of. Old story, open the can.

In 1983, a Japanese artist, Tadahiko Ogawa, made a copy of the Mona Lisa completely out of ordinary toast. There was a football player for the New York Giants with the nickname "Toast" because he was burned all the time for touchdowns. So, what? Toast. Crossing one's fingers is a way of secretly making the sign of the Cross. It was started by early Christians to ask for divine assistance without attracting the attention of pagans. Crossing the toes is a way of secretly making sure you are still alive, the rare ability to actually cross your toes saying more than I can possibly say. A baby octopus is about the size of a flea when it is born. I once saw a flea the size of an octopus, but it was dead. A slug has four noses. My memories have one nose. 62 degrees Fahrenheit is the minimum temperature required for a grasshopper to be able to hop. I have a brass statue of a grasshopper in my office, but it doesn't do me any good because the wise man called me once and said "Grasshopper" and the awful world showed up, instead. Fine-grained volcanic ash can be found as an ingredient in some toothpaste. So can blood. Some asteroids have other asteroids orbiting them. Some hemorrhoids have other hemorrhoids orbiting them. Devoid of its cells and proteins, human blood has the same general makeup as sea water. I prefer the river.

HIT THE FLOOR

In the fifth grade, we hit the floor under our desks or huddled against the walls of the classroom when the drill sounded. Red Russian bombs were coming. Atomic fallout was going to rain down from the desert sky and disrupt our learning day. We knelt under our desks and put our arms over our heads, crouching low like scared rabbits upon the teacher's command. Maybe the bombs were too powerful for a desk, so the week after, we switched to sitting our little asses against the brick walls in the hallway, the school made to withstand anything, the mushroom cloud not daring to sweep through the hallway to take us away. We sat in two long rows of puzzled kids facing each other, the occasional giggle or fart echoing down the corridor as the teachers marched between us, their sacrifice if hell came not apparent, though a teacher's pet or two raised a hand to ask where their favorite teacher was going to sit. Someone once cried out, "Hit the floor!" Everyone laughed, the siren the principal played over the loudspeaker stopping suddenly that day. Silence followed and everyone was frozen scared, one teacher commanding, "Get down lower, Fred. Sally, pull that skirt over your legs." We pushed our backs harder against the bricks, kept our legs locked together as we bent at the waist, folded into defiant bodies who knew how to radiate resistance, smart enough to know the Russians would never get us because we were chosen patriots, though we had no clue we could become part of our beloved school building, possibly melt into the bricks, our daily practice of learning how to avoid evaporation perhaps a parody of those black and white films of Hiroshima survivors that our teacher never dared to show when she told us to raise our heads and open our American history books.

HAIR BALL

One of my cats hurled a hair ball as big as a hot dog onto the carpet.
As I cleaned it up, trying not to hurl myself, I realized I was in the right
place at the right time, though my wife would claim I am not good at
cleaning such a mess. After painting one of his last masterpieces, Picasso turned to a friend and muttered, "All art is the art of destruction."
I shrugged as I stared at the mess on the floor, then looked out my office window in time to witness a male duck attack another male, mating
season and territorial quackings echoing across the yard until the two
ducks flew away in a swirl of wings and feathers. I knelt on the carpet
and grabbed the hair ball with a paper towel, felt a reaction in my gut
and hurried to the trash can in the laundry room. I dumped it there
and washed my hands, the stain on the carpet making me think of Hart
Crane, who once wrote, "There are no trophies of the sun." I had no idea
what that meant until another morning thunderstorm shook the house
and the two-minute hail storm bounced in the yard, balls of ice disappearing as quickly as they fell.

By the time it was over, I had sprayed and wiped the carpet and my cat
was hiding, its tiny presence somewhere in the house bringing Kenneth Rexroth to mind. He whispered once, "I am startled until I realize
that the beehive in the hollow trunk of the tree will be busy all night."
I thought about such a sound in the quiet room and wondered what it
had to do with cleaning a hairball, so I sat in my favorite recliner and
waited for the cat to reappear. I wanted to hold it in my arms, but the
cat knew what it had done and left me there waiting, its refusal to show
itself bringing a note from one of my favorite Marianne Faithfull songs
where she cries, "There are many caves I could choose to live in." I sat
there and waited as Marianne climbed through her song, then I noticed a
yellow stain on the carpet from the hair ball.

THE SMALL SEARCHLIGHT

The small searchlight comes out of nowhere and scans my brain. When I open my eyes, it is yesterday and I am innocent of every crime, the beam searching that far back to see what makes me afraid. The light explores all possibilities, even takes apart my desert landscape and rearranges it to resemble the planet Mars. The searchlight pinpoints the places where I refuse to go, or even think about, areas of my guilty life silhouetted in the stark beam, my secrets and hidden ideas refusing the illumination, this small light acting as if probing is everything—all matter and existence narrowed down to a touch of fire directed from unknown sources, my attempts to dodge it futile because the laser is already inside my head and escape would mean I would not be there the moment the torch lights the fuse and I become a different man.

DADA MEANS ELEPHANT

After Francis Picabia

Dada means elephant when the large animal puts on its diaper and sig-
nals to the world it is ready to negotiate. This brings out the ghosts of
men with extremely large hands who go about massaging the backs of
rare birds they carry in cages designed to look like falling stars gathered
right after they hit the earth without exploding, though map 48 shows
they have destroyed the wrong planet that actually is encased in a locket
each of these men wear around their necks. When this is discovered,
mud wasps abandon the ears of the elephant and swarm until they be-
come invisible, this thought growing a hair inside the nose of the grand
inquisitor who survives the stampede and adores his porno collection
locked inside a golden trunk. This creates expeditions into the art of
deconstruction, though the language involved has no word for elephant
or for the contemplation of awareness and deception—key tools the el-
ephant uses in formulating why the shower in the bathroom won't turn
off or why the female elephant doesn't climb out of there. Dada pauses
here to announce the constipation of solidified ideas was originally
intended for horizontal people who wear space and factory chemicals
quite well, their relationships with the sweltering dusk often making
fine research projects for hunters returning from failed attempts at
capping the elephant that shed its diaper a long time ago. At this point,
Dada involves water, and the rain that paints blind men is the water
long anticipated as the cure for self-deception, meaningless abstraction,
and tremendous manipulation of the circus flower found lodged in the
left foot of the suffering elephant that has been screaming for its dead
babies, the memory of them dying in the jungle encased in some bone
dream a legendary explorer will find two days before it runs out of wa-
ter in the middle of the wilderness. Dada used to mean elephant when
the large animal waited for the results of its pregnancy test and aban-
doned all hope of conquering the world when the negative results came
back.

SCRATCH

He scratched but it wouldn't go away. He scratched again, but couldn't get rid of it, the motion of scratching making him scratch even more until the idea of scratching overtook him and he learned the art of scratching. When he paused for air, the movements he went through brought the desire to scratch again, but he fought the urge. He gave in and had to scratch at the exact pinpoint that focused on fire and reaction.

This made him crazy, but there was a layer to the idea of a scratch that went beyond red skin and kept him alive through the ordeal, the color of his body changing as he dug deeper into his soul to find the origin of the disturbance that made him a veteran scratcher. His fingernails were dull since he clipped them days ago. When he extracted the source of his attention, he did it by scratching, but it was the kind of digging with short nails that kept men alive, though the torture was a lesson in the tradition of scratching.

As he scratched, his face was distorted, his arms and legs flailing with each turn. He saw this excavation of the body as a necessary elevation in what made him scratch, the layer of sensitivity raising him to the level of a burning god, forcing him to understand the highest state of perception, the plains of sore heaven creating the need to scratch by planting the eternal itch that makes men move.

Yet, as he scratched and rode the torture to hallucinatory moments, he realized it was more than an itch. It could not be labeled an itch. Instead, the action uncovered an entrance to the self that wanted extraction and was attempting to take the shortest and most uncomfortable way to becoming the needle of ascension and worship.

He scratched to find his identity and to bolster his will to block its exit. In defying the course of things in his body, he scratched too far. Before he knew it, the scratch had become everything and he was both the violator and the savior—a circling of the senses that drove him to scratch his existence inside and out, this erosion transforming him into a legend—a bloody notion and the exact thought, that infamous flame residing on the other side of reconstruction.

I SMELL

I smell the murals of Diego Rivera and the burning guitar of Jimi Hendrix, smell the fish Christ refused at the feast and the beer breath of my grandfather, dead 62 years, the flowers at my grandmother's funeral and the last meal my father ate before he abandoned my mother. I smell the smoke of an extinct volcano and the paint on the face of Moctezuma, the open hands on the outstretched arms of La Virgen de Guadalupe and the jet fuel of our worst nightmares.

I smell the stinking feet of my father at the end of his working day and the electric wires behind my computer, the oily rag Miles Davis used to shine his trumpet and the polish on John Coltrane's shoes. I can still smell the perfume of my first girlfriend in high school, the desert after a quiet rain, the mud on the drowned man pulled out of the Rio Grande and the incense in Chairman Mao's private brothel.

I smell the onion of Miguel Hernandez's starving son and the holy water of the last church I set foot in, the sweat of the son I never had, the clay on Alberto Giacometti's hands, the gunpowder on the Border Patrolman's pistol and the plums William Carlos Williams wanted to eat.

I smell the shit of the parrot I had when I was four years old, along with the scent of the wet feather that fell on my sleeping head, the sulfur of the ghost I can never see, the dark room where my grandmother died, the empty canyon I couldn't climb and the seashells in Pablo Neruda's house, the engine of the car that took me away from El Paso for good.

I smell the dust on the yellow family photos from 1923 and the last bath I took before I grew up, the plaster on the death mask of Pancho Villa, the mosquito repellent I used when I finally climbed the canyon and wrinkled my nose at the clear air before a rattlesnake struck.

I smell the ink on the typewriters where I wrote my first poems and the glue in my old scrapbook of rejection slips, the shampooed hair of the woman who loves me and the trash can where I threw away notes no one could read, the tortured feet of San Martin de Porres, the glowing ashes of a fallen saint.

I smell the first snow I ever saw in my life and the summer grass of a house where I never belonged, the lightning that hit the tree half a block from my childhood home, fumes of a life I would live.

DISTRUST CREATION

A fifty-four-year-old man appears out of nowhere and thinks he hears music in the air. The world of sound has been hiding inside iPods and headphones for years, so he is stunned to hear electric beats tear the sun with wild guitars and unstoppable drums. A man looks about and wants to find the source of the music because it is moving him and he wants to dance across the brightly lit field in front of him, the grass freshly mowed as if some concert is about to happen across its gentle slopes. A man steps forward and is overcome by dizziness, the green at his feet spinning rapidly and making him fall. He hits the fine turf, smells the grass for an instant and drums explode, their cymbals crashing in his ears because the long solo is about to begin.

This man is young and nineteen years old, sitting on the hard concrete floor of the arena, thousands of stoned freaks jumping and screaming, surrounding him with cannabis sweat and the steady roar of psychedelic anticipation, his friends swaying and shaking their long hair, Blues Image about to start the show as the opening act for The Steve Miller Band and Santana, a concert the man has been looking forward to for weeks. The man is high and flying, the immense lights in the arena breaking and flashing as the show begins and joint after joint is passed back and forth, the lights going down into a swimming purple that covers the stage as the guitarists rip the air apart and the lead singer starts screaming. A man knows where he is going and this man sits between his buzzing friends, tasting everything that is handed to him.

The man hits the ground of the future at the same instant he hits the concrete of the past when everything goes black before Blues Image can finish the second song. He wakes up alone, the huge arena empty and deeply silent, though its acres of concrete floor are covered in trash—cups of Coke, pieces of clothing, half-eaten hot-dogs, cigarette butts and splashes of vomit painting the floor. You name it and it has been left behind by the thousands who loved the great show. A man lies with his swollen face on the concrete, but spots the tiny figure of a janitor pushing a broom about one hundred yards away, the mountain of post-concert garbage a true challenge as the janitor sweeps acres of arena floor. A man sits up alone and doesn't quite know where he is. His head hurts and his mouth is cotton dry. He turns to the stage and it is empty, the instruments and drums taken away, the mikes torn down hours ago. The last thing he recalls is hitting the eighth or ninth fat joint before passing it on, the guitarist for Blues Image burning something inside the man's ears before everything went dark.

This man appears out of nowhere and he hears music in the air. The concert arena is empty and the show is over. He struggles to get up from the concrete, hoping to get out of there before the huge steel doors are closed forever. He thinks he hears music in the air. The world of sound has been hiding in the silent ears of the world in recent years and he hasn't heard any live music in decades. He sits up in the smooth grass and shakes his head in bright sunlight. As he looks across the field, rows of automatic sprinklers come on and start to soak him. Trying to rise, he slips and falls in the watery turf. He gets up again. As he rises, a black iPod in his shirt pocket slips out, but he catches it in mid-air before its fragile glass face hits the wet ground and explodes.

FINDINGS (1)

Scientists have discovered that baboons fall in love. A research lab in Truth or Consequences, New Mexico, observed microscopic robots growing in a petry dish, the tiny machines filling the container within minutes, their flashing lights observable only through high-powered microscopes. Doctors found the root of a tomato plant growing on the left leg of a twelve-year-old boy in the San Luis Valley of Colorado. When he was brought into the town clinic, a half-inch green bud was sticking out of his skin. Surgery removed the entire plant. Scientists observed a rattlesnake swim for two days inside a glass tank, until it floated on the surface in exhaustion. It took another four hours for the snake to drown. Analyzing the water in the tank revealed it had become a powerful truth serum. Scientists in government labs continue to drown rattlesnakes and send the water to military agencies for their secret interrogations of suspected terrorists. A lab technician in Ann Arbor, Michigan accidentally tied a copper wire to the wrong leg of a chicken skeleton, a fragile frame completely stripped of meat. When he punched codes into his laptop screen, the chicken vaporized, though the data recorded by the use of the wrong wire resulted in a new software program that destroys computer viruses instantly. Most ducks in wilderness ponds prefer cloudy days to clear sunny ones for laying their eggs. The majority of ducks studied in city parks and in other metropolitan bodies of water laid more eggs on sunny days.

People with many children are more likely to have pleasant dreams than nightmares. People with less than two children have more nightmares. Childless couples were not studied. Scientists in Texas recently cloned a Great Horned Owl. Coffee makes eyelashes on humans grow faster. Researchers in Detroit, Michigan successfully used DNA to create a functional self-assembling electronic car engine. Pulp from pink Valentine's Day envelopes, uncovered in an attic box from 1954, was mixed with fresh pulp to make computer printer paper. When the paper plant pressed the new sheets, they came out pink without colored ink added to the process. Forty reams of pink paper were produced this way. Researchers in California taught genetically engineered smallpox to communicate using a new chemical language. The original research was aimed at creating tiny robots, but government programs are exploring ways to create microscopic, talking soldiers whose chemical make-up is made of nothing but intelligent strains of smallpox. It was discovered that bats in Carlsbad Caverns, New Mexico feed on peyote plants that grow abundantly in the desert surrounding the national park. European researchers announced that nude sunbathers give off a different aura, captured on computer film, than sunbathers wearing bathing suits. This was found to be true for both men and women. Scientists recently said that synthetic trout eat an average of twelve pounds more of various kinds of bait, including worms. Astronomers suggested that Earth might be shedding a new kind of light toward space. The origins of these new beams center at both the North and South Pole, but scientists are not sure if the observed lights are a natural phenomena or whether they are man-made because recent studies have found massive traces of highly concentrated uranium in the energy of the lights. It was found that sixty-five percent of lifelines on the palms of left-handed humans were longer than on the palms of right-handed people.

Affordable Aphorisms

The man with a prayer book is the man lost at sea.

The chirping of the morning bird is what you never dreamed last night.

When you add up the coins in your pocket, the total is worth more when you miscount.

If you had a normal childhood, your biographers will label it The Age of Reason.

If you grew up in a dysfunctional family, your secrets are the first flowers to grow in the first house you will own as an adult.

The first ghost you spot crossing the road will always cross toward the east.

The man who owns more than one hat is the man who lessens his ability to think.

To recognize yourself in a Hollywood movie is to pretend there is more than one world.

One is not condemned to be a character in a children's cartoon unless one is a true adult.

To be "nude at the wrong beach" is final proof there is more than one world.

The mosquito on the naked arm is a sign you have been distracted for too many years.

To name at least six obscure paintings in the museum is to haunt the life of the painters in previous incarnations you never knew about.

The man who prefers the end crust of a loaf of bread is the man who goes to bed early.

The man who prefers the inside of the loaf is the man who struggles to stay up late.

The man who refuses any part of the loaf is the man who dwells past midnight.

To dream of large breasts every night is to miss the days of enclosed public telephone booths.

You can tell a parrot anything.

Two moments of inattention per day is punishment for having too many enemies.

To spit on the bedroom wall is to deny love at any cost.

To spit on the bathroom floor is to deny good luck at any cost.

To spit into one's own open palm is to accept the mighty truth.

At the end of sunny days, heaven comes down and cries on the earth.

At the end of cloudy days, dreamers and sinners look up to the sky.

Driftwood in the river is the remains of a castle never conquered.

The clown mask in the window always scares the bravest children.

To wear the clown mask is to deny a political situation.

Two pancakes in the morning are worth more than two chicken drumsticks at night.

To exile yourself in writing is to wear the wrong deodorant for years.

One apple in the hand is better than two oranges between your feet.

A book of poems can be read upside down.

A book of fiction must always be right side up.

It doesn't matter how you read a book of non-fiction.

To wake early is to deny there are dark streets outside.

To sleep in late is to deny there is sunlight outside.

James Wright Returns to Minneapolis

I spotted him on the corner of Lake and Cedar, the cemetery across the road streaked with snow, its gravestones surrounded by a black fence that kept anyone from seeing what was really there. James Wright was back in Minneapolis, waiting for the bus to St. Paul. I pulled over and parked my car, got out and waited for the light to turn green. He stared straight ahead and grew smaller in his coat as I approached.

We stood alone at the bus stop as I said, "James, James Wright?" He turned to me and I saw the scar at his throat, white whiskers frozen to his face, his poem about the Indian with a hook for a hand coming to me as he shook his head without a word. "James, it's you," I said and wanted to hug him. A bus passed, but it wasn't the right one and he looked down at his dirty shoes like a professor caught in some act.

"James, what are you doing here?" I asked. He looked up at me and pushed his eyeglasses farther on his nose. "Do you remember when I waited for the bus and the Indian came by and dropped a coin into my paw?" I said nothing because it was that poem. James smiled to himself and shrugged. "I forgot to thank him," he told me. "I got on the bus without saying goodbye."

I didn't know what to say and stood there with James Wright, his poem trying to take this encounter away. We waited for his bus in silence, but it never came. He waved off each one that passed by, acting as if I wasn't there. "Can I give you a ride?" I finally asked. James Wright turned to me and whispered, "That's what did it. The guy had a hook." He held his bare, right hand up in the cold air, reached into his left coat pocket with the other hand and gave me a dollar bill. "Goodbye," he said and I took the money as James Wright started walking toward Minneapolis, his back turned to the rows of the dead.

LET ME DISAPPEAR

According to scientists, astronauts get taller when they are in space and in Albania, nodding your head means "no" and shaking your head means "yes." This says I am going to disappear and become a parrot, sitting on my perch in some strange woman's living room, ready to imitate everything she has to say to her illicit lover over the phone. Maybe I won't have to speak in the shrill voice of parrots, but simply nod and shake my head, getting it right, unlike the Albanians. St. Paul, Minnesota was originally called Pig's Eye after a man named Pierre "Pig's Eye" Parrant who set up the first business there in the mid-nineteenth century. Well, let me disappear because I live about twelve miles south of St. Paul's southern city limits and have seen the eyes of pigs quite often. Minnesota is full of them. The last one I saw was tailgating me and almost ran me off the road. Before I could switch lanes, he swerved around me and shot away. About four blocks later, he was pulled over by a cop and given a ticket. Astronaut Buzz Aldrin's mother's maiden name was "Moon." That sentence is hard to say. Of course, Buzz was the second man to step onto the moon in 1969. The first was Neil Armstrong, but he had no moons in his family, so he pleaded to Buzz on his knees, "Please, let me go second. Let me go second and every moon lover will love you forever, instead of me." This happened inside the capsule on its way down to the moon. Buzz thought, "Let me disappear," but it was too late. They hit the surface and history was on its way. I don't have a clue what this has to do with me because the only moon in my life rose over the desert skies for the first twenty-five years of my life, until I disappeared. It is why I insist on a dark, moonless night when it is the best time for all men to go away, inspect their dreams, and maybe come back taller, wiser, and able to know the difference between yes and no.

THE CROSS

Most days, I don't think about it or see it. Sometimes, I notice the Christ on the wall and the dark wood of the crucifix, perhaps the cross that crossed a moment of faith years ago, but is now an image that fades in and out of my life. Most years, I pray to things I don't know I am praying to, though I could examine them and find the twisted stick figure I pulled out of the river, or a broken seashell, perhaps the skeleton of a lizard that turned to dust in my dreams, even the rosary whose red beads were pressed from rose petals in Spain and given to me by my grandmother before she died, the sweet aroma of death trapped inside the tiny white box it came in.

Is there anything wrong with moving silently toward those things without seeing the cross in front of me, that symbol, the hanging and its sacrifice that hung from every room in every house where I grew up? Most hours, the shape gets closer and I can't admit that the things we were told to believe in as children are the things that will meet us at the gate. Our beliefs were chosen for us.

The cross is the marker for choices that were made in our baptized name. The cross is the unknown that becomes a mystery because, wanting it or not, it has become a part of us. Someone dying with his feet hanging off the ground supposedly showed us it is acceptable to be lifted off the earth. Ascension and the cross. Ascension and the symbol of +.

What does this mean? Will confession and forced communion solve everything? Most days, I accept the fact I carry the Catholic seed that won't leave my brain, though I don't want to believe it. The cross may not help me find out why. It may only make me wonder how young I was on the day I swallowed it completely and the cross formed the crossroads in my throat that lead in two directions and allow me, on some days, to stand at the black intersection and look both ways.

MY STONE, MY MASK

I eat white bones, splinters for a blessing. Crushed and swallowing, I am strong, the robed instructor in how to grow wings and pursue the guitar chord stuck in the throat. Deeply, I consume a cruel thought that I have forgotten something, placed the wrong profile in front of my face, bright heaven of masks buying me time to lose those who wanted to learn from me.

I caress the ribbed membrane of an exotic fish, swallow a second that hurts, then spit the table out of my mouth—its plain, its horizon, the flat table where we used to sit together and eat. I grind up old chairs in my teeth, imagine what it is like to breathe at once, be full together, plan the coldness of the night where the stone is pushed across the floor.

I bite my tongue accidentally, hurt my mouth before finding a space to change my looks, the unfinished setting of white silk resembling the bed of the faithful wife who painted masks on a thousand men, her presence giving me a second chance to wash my face, remove the stone from between my eyes as if this would make me open them and understand.

You Got the Spider

The first satellite pictures from the unseen side of Mercury reveal the wrinkles of a shrinking, aging planet with scars from volcanic eruptions and a birthmark shaped like a spider. The ancient spider appears on news websites, the black and white photograph from outer space revealing how the spider made it from Mercury to my heart, where a spider has resided for my fifty-five years. I know this because I grew up in the land of tarantulas and used to stand in the desert and watch them crawl around my ankles. I had no fear of them as a boy and I know one of them, somehow, crawled up my legs and into my heart. I have written about this before, but I keep going back to the "birthmark."

The god of Mercury born as a spider and allowing a man with a spider in his heart to gaze at him from millions of miles away. The question, of course, is what is a spider doing in my heart? Proponents of spiders in the heart insist a man with a spider in his chest goes in unexpected directions so he can live how he wants to live, allowing his imagination to crawl through his brain. His arterial spider legs beat beyond the atmosphere of Mercury to keep blood rhythm from staring at the universe, the boy allowing tarantulas to trace patterns over his feet until the ruins of yesterday are overrun with spiders.

PART 2

THE SKY IS BEAUTIFUL

The sky is beautiful but few thoughts reach it. On days the war continues, the sky adjusts by moving south, leaving a duplicate blue revolving above the heads of those who have the talent to notice, though their silence grows deep. On days the war attempts to end, nothing happens, so the killing continues under the beautiful sky that forgives smoke and kisses helicopters on their way down. The sky is there but few enraged moments reach it because the surge includes magnificent clouds and miles of untouched blue.

On the surface of a cloud, a color passes and bleeds a headline only the blind can read. When weather becomes a factor, the individual who is tracking this gets ill and has to go home. The sky remains what it is and will change the language of our hidden nature when the blue horizon finally touches the other blue horizon and dangerous events stop taking place. The sky is beautiful but this observation is meant for those who truly care about the fate of the air and the continent and the breathing space that grows smaller as the explosions echo across the sea.

When the damage gets closer, the inclusion of the sky as a character in this becomes clear and this stops the talented observer in his tracks. He must have never made it home because his house is silhouetted beneath the loveliest blue he has ever seen, a hue that makes him drop his notes and surrender. The sky is beautiful as the sun goes down and this burning is the last thing left alive when night enters the picture and the black sky, filled with overconfident stars, lays a beautiful blanket over the war and the dying twenty-year-olds. The sky is beautiful for the simple reason that what happens underneath it every day first took place in the drama of heaven where they say there is no sky.

ALTERNATIVE SIMILARITY

What do we do with an episode of alternative similarity where all things are the same? When we open our eyes, what we see is what we see. We close our eyes and nothing changes. If we believe both worlds are the same, what is the point of exploration and how can we get to the dark spot that has tugged on our shirts for years? What do we do with an episode of the straight highway staying straight as it enters the mountains? There might be something wrong with the way things unfold before us and we miss the shadow box that hovers above our heads as we wake each morning. Yet, the highway passes straight through the mountains. If things could possibly change and form two very different worlds, that would be the moment to be brave and run to some place where we have not been before. In the end, we might be accused of trying to be someone or something we are not. If so, who would be making the accusations?

Paleoanthropologists announced the discovery of a species of hobbit-like humans on Flores, an island 370 miles east of Bali. The adult hobbits, who lived as recently as 13,000 years ago, were about the size of a three-year-old modern human child and they hunted pygmy elephants and Komodo dragons. Could this be a source of an alternative similarity? The dragons are still out there and no one is hunting them because the hunter is now the dragon and the hobbit world is a fantasy on DVD screens that pull the realities of the past into alternatives that blend escape with the violent world of our ancestors. But, is this about our familial past? No, it is about the hobbit possibilities that shrink the human capacity for destruction into three-foot dragon killers that rewrote myths and tales that lie buried somewhere on that island near Bali.

If alternative similarity is at play, then it is time to admit that the new species of "fearless mouse" scientists recently created will serve a purpose outside of the test tube. When the scientists made this announcement, they threw in the opinion that the earth is unlikely to be destroyed any time soon. So, it may give the fearless mouse time to find something it can fear. This alternative to years of hard work in creating a rodent who is not afraid of anything might be the way out of this. The other choice that presents itself comes from our beloved desert home-land, where brown pelicans were observed to be crashing into streets in Tucson, Arizona because the heat waves of summer rising from the pavement looked like water. What are pelicans doing in the desert and why are they brown? Is this an alternative to the expected white bird of green forests and wilderness rivers? Yet, the desert is a rich ecosystem where pine forests and glacial movements can be found. This doesn't help the poor city pelican who smashes into the 110 degree heat of the asphalt in Tucson. This adds to the road kill count, but the pelican wasn't run over. It flew on its own into an alternative similarity that gave no warning as it drew the poor bird to the ground.

It is tempting to separate pelican actions from fearless mice and hobbit people, yet they weave together when similarities remain hidden until someone reveals what has been uncovered. The reality is that conclusions about the steady mouse, the dumb pelicans, and the evaporation of dragon-hunting dwarfs have vanished from the human brain. Exploration and discovery are gone because tragic consequences entered the mind of the researcher and destroyed what was found. The person chosen to pronounce the secret behind these alternative similarities stares with a blank expression across a vast sea of doubt. The asphalt is cool under his feet, there are no rodents upon the clean stage, and the only midgets he has known were the bullies in his sixth grade class who pounded on him on the playground during lunch. This triumph of fusing knowledge out of various states of awareness is obvious as the person is finally led off the stage because a highway is continuously passing through mountains that surround the city where he was going to make his pronouncement.

What do we do with alternative similarity where all things are the same and no one discovers how to change them? Why did human thought evaporate? When we open our eyes, what we see is what we see. We close our eyes and nothing changes. The mousetraps are empty, the birds are near a faraway river, and the dragons keep circling the house. If we believe there is more than one world, what is the point of exploration and how can we get to that dark spot that has tugged on our shirts for years? What do we do with an episode of the straight highway staying straight as it enters the mountains and we don't look back because our brains, that let us down when it came to alternative similarities, are now thinking about ice cream and finding a gas station in the middle of nowhere?

IT COULD BE A SONG

It could be a song, but is only a late night radio show playing songs from 1967, tripping out the old farts who live in a time warp of the heart, their minds psychedelicized decades ago with The Jefferson Airplane, Strawberry Alarm Clock, Blues Magoos, The Mothers of Invention, The Grateful Dead—masters of trip out songs that weave the aging brain into a dance of lights, sound, and waves that space the brain for a lifetime, popping over the air from time to time in celebration of the idea that true hippies never grow old.

It could be a song, but what does it mean to have sixties music elongate the head and heart, stretching the power of memory with the beat of colors and smells and smoke, not forgetting the lights and purple and red eyes, the banners and fog, the band and the feedback—things in the mind and body forever, though it could be a song that pulls us to the space where we go back and never quite get there because we are already there and have been there since 1967, never moving from the moment when Quicksilver Messenger Service, Country Joe and the Fish, and Moby Grape burned something in our skulls that cannot be erased, though this party marking the years is an attempt to burn it again.

These songs are being played forty years after they exploded on the walls because we can't forget as we use the latest sound technology, vinyl spinning on an old turntable abandoned decades ago because the radio is on the computer and The 13th Floor Elevators, Love, The Chambers Brothers, and Buffalo Springfield are streamed beyond the mind of excursion and recollection—the electric soul that integrates ancient rock somewhere in the body where it beats forever. Forty years after, it could be a song, but it has become an electric blood cell plugged into the amplifier of the heart where a journey within and outside the human form turns into endless feedback.

21ST CENTURY FRIEND

First, let's not get carried away. Mercy is rare and the defeated run in circles, insisting their day will come. The standard marker is always a tree, blind with emotion and leaves, their caring shade expecting us to play out our fantasies among the branches.

Second, the mind says one thing, but the bow and arrow are encased in glass, expecting history to dance. Let's pass out flags, carry buckets of water, and protect our children from alien diseases because we found UFOs in our back pockets.

Let's insist the cell phone will ring and bring hope because the justice in its tone will change the theory of the Apostles and their miraculous greed, Jesus still waiting to unplug his phone charger from the wall.

His way out is lined with bricks, manifestos, and the unraveling demon splashed on the walls, yet we can't stop and stare at the meaning of this. Things will come to pass in our fresh and violent century, so let us see how resistance is revelation and those are moments we are going to grab with fists.

I Used to Be Bob Dylan

I used to be Bob Dylan when I was young and thought I could sing and change the world. I used to be Zimmerman and knew every secret of political and cultural America, churning out the keys to social change on my poorly tuned acoustic guitar. I convinced my friends I came from upper Minnesota and my parents were jewel thieves who where struck by lightning one day and wound up rich and anonymous in Florida. I used to be Dylan in the days of danger and doubt, small crowds loving me, many women taking me away, though I can only innuendo on that in song. I used to be Dylan when I gave up on being John Lennon—probably the biggest tragedy in rock, but my sunglasses keep me from going into that. The underground films captured it, though it was hard to be me in the past. The subterranean life became the style of the rich and touched, though I was the only true American artist who gave and gave, then took it away for his own use. All I'm saying is being Dylan was how I wrote classic tunes and my old costume brought it and took it away. I am not Bobby in the present and there is no point in talking about what I can't be tomorrow. I used to be him and had the world as a stage before I got too famous for my own good. I'm not putting myself down because I'm not him anymore and Bobby can do whatever he wants. He's done it all and smoked it all, tucked it in and I used to be him when I made up songs on the spot in my smoky hotel room, Joan baby by my side. I used to be Dylan when it paid to be someone like him, loving and worshipping me because I had the palest skin this side of Rimbaud. I could strap on my electric Fender and eat up the boos and hisses from the crowd, those days of lust and awe having the power to get me past the spotlight because I used to be Dylan when being Dylan was the same thing as being myself.

ERASE THE SEVENTH MOON

Erase the seventh moon and you will be rewarded with the madness of an open mouth. Take away the seventh white ball and you shall be granted a sugar cube for the sake of research. Wipe out the full seventh house in the sky and claim your only religion is the invisible one you swallow each time you breathe. Erase the moon after the sixth and you will be rewarded with the floor of composition where a black cat runs across the surface and you follow it across the universe, until you realize you haven't left the room.

Erase the seventh moon from your secret notebooks and your desires will be noted as forever's violin, the instrument traced on the craters visible from the eye, instrument lodged in your head by a fleeing man who came by to see you quiver. Destroy the quarter slice of the fire before the eighth ball that falls to earth and you will surrender pink steam that floats down from the last explorer who came up with an answer for this.

Erase the seventh moon from train tracks that never went, the journey postponed by the dark city that wasn't there. Evaporate the seventh flower and forget how it grew out of what you never had, what pushed you to reach above your head and pluck the moon away from its myth, its dangling light kissing the infection and the human right, bringing you familiar war greetings from those who survived their own acts of erasure.

PABLO PICASSO SPIT IN MY FACE

Pablo Picasso spit in my face and told me I was no artist. He said he had to hold onto the great secrets and I had no choice but to settle for weakness and bouts of crying. He put his arm around my shoulders after spitting on me and led me to the door of his studio, the incredible smell of acrylic paint making me dizzier than the spit of a genius running down my forehead. Before he let me go, he whispered that it was good for some of us to weep and struggle in the darkness. I nodded as if I understood and wiped the last of his fluid off my face. He closed the door to his studio quietly and went back to work. I climbed down the stone stairs, unfolded my huge wings and flew away.

FINDINGS (2)

When millions of cicadas emerge across the eastern United States for a rare mating season, they will appear as tasty morsels to pets that could get sick from eating the insects, officials warned. The insects are protein-rich but their hard outer shells can cause vomiting and constipation in cats and dogs. Scientists also report that the oil from fingerprints on electric guitars will eventually change the sound of the instruments, even causing them to go out of tune over a period of time and creating short-circuits in the electrical system inside the body of the guitars. Researchers discovered that a tiny grooming instrument, used to trim nose hairs, leaves metallic shavings in the nostrils each time the user turns the tiny teeth in the device. Heart surgeons in Chicago found eight undissolved cholesterol pills blocking a man's heart valves when they opened him up. If you take four cups of green tea and mix them with one quart of car engine oil, the resulting liquid can power a lawn mower for six months. Scientists at the University of Ohio crossed geranium plants with bluebells. The plant that grew as a result had deep black petals on circular blossoms and a sticky red colored resin seeped out of the plant. Scientists in both California and Russia claim to have achieved miniature nuclear explosions inside condoms made from the stomach linings of sharks.

When a U.S. Wildlife team reached the top of a peak in Alaska, they found a frozen lake with several dozen old horseshoes embedded in the ice. South Korean scientists formed thirty new strains of DNA when they cloned panda bear embryos from the stem cells of condors and boa constrictors. The British Medical Association recently reported that smoking cigarettes stops fingernails from growing, while smoking marijuana makes ingrown toenails go deeper into the skin. Marital beds facing east windows make married couples have sex more often. Marital beds facing west make them have infrequent sex. Eight volunteers in a lab study ate a blended combination of chicken hearts, oatmeal, catsup, crushed Twinkies, raw squid, and horseradish for one week. No one threw up, only two disliked the taste, and all eight reported a higher rate of recalling their dreams in the morning. Engineers discovered microscopic cracks in solar panels that powered a fish hatchery in Oregon caused extra sunlight to filter into the growing tanks. The results were that several hundred trout with three eyes hatched for several days. Psychologists in a special study in Manhattan found that people who crossed against red lights had more confidence in their working environments and made higher salaries than those who waited for green lights before crossing. They also found higher mortality rates among those crossing against the red lights. Skunks urinate more often than porcupines. Electric guitars for left-handed players blow fuses more often than common right-handed guitars. An average of four hummingbird eggs fit inside the normal human belly-button.

CHURCH

A man walks into a church and finds he is the only person in the dark sanctuary. He goes to the altar where several votive candles are quietly burning. He stops in front of a peeling statue of La Virgen de Guadalupe, bows down before the shrine and makes the sign of the cross. Suddenly, a bat flies out of nowhere and streaks across the chamber. Startled, he follows the darting creature with his eyes as it disappears beyond the choir balcony. He turns back to the candles so he can pray, but is disrupted by a drop of water landing on his sleeve. He looks up at the distant ceiling in time for a second drop to hit him on the chin. It's raining outside and the roof is leaking. The man moves on his knees a couple of feet down the bench and begins his first Our Father. He is halfway through the prayer when an altar boy, mumbling incoherently, runs from the priest's chamber, his footsteps echoing through the church. The man is distracted again as the boy, dressed in his colorful frock, takes one of the small burning candles and returns to the back room. The man shakes his head at the trail of wax the boy drips on the floor. This time, he manages a complete Our Father and two Hail Marys before a dense cloud of incense fills the air around the statue. He begins to cough and his eyes start burning.

He rises to his feet and notices the poison sweetness of the incense is coming from the priest's chamber. He coughs and walks back there, but the incense makes him nauseous and he stops at the door. Inside, the altar boy is holding the ugly bat over the candle flame, its wings folded so it won't escape. Next to him, an old priest is crying and shaking his head, his clothes soaked from the rain, a pot of incense hanging from a rope in his outstretched hand. The man turns and bolts down the long aisle between the pews. As he reaches the sanctuary doors, he spots the containers of holy water mounted on the walls. He can't resist and dips a finger in one of them, then raises the wet finger to trace a cross on his forehead. This sets off a loud clattering of wings behind him, but he does not turn to look. When he opens the door, it is early evening and the rain has stopped, everything under the sky wet and shiny. Hundreds of bats pour out of an open window below the bell tower. They fill the sky as the man stands under the arch, not quite sure where he parked his car. Three more altar boys come up the concrete stairs toward him and he gets out of the way as two priests embrace each other on the sidewalk near the street.

EASTER

The guitars are quiet because the candles have a journey today. They dream of resurrection in a time of war and savagery, the terror of the tombs passing its silence across the seas that have become bridges to nowhere. People are alive. People are dead and the cross shadows its own history as it heads east and becomes invisible, its transparent weapons ready to wipe out any resistance.

What does this have to do with a pink or green or blue plastic Easter egg?

A favorite rock critic writes, "Turning 50. It's a daunting prospect for anyone (and I should know). But for a pop song? Most fade away long before they reach that mark. One exception: the legendary 'Louie Louie' — that eternally youthful 1960s garage-rock anthem first recorded exactly 50 years ago this month. Far from shuffling off to a quiet retirement, evidence indicates that 'Louie Louie' may actually prove to be immortal."

The nuggets of time and the guitars are still quiet. Who knows how long this will last because the box set called Nuggets contains four CDs of classic garage rock, songs from high school that meant something in the days when high school meant there was sound in the air, even if it wasn't inside the head yet.

True Nugget oldies from the box set, played over and over in the time of the quiet guitars:

"She's About a Mover," by The Sir Douglas Quintet; "You Must be a Witch," by The Lollipop Shoppe; "Put the Clock Back on the Wall," by The "E" Types; "Journey to the Center of the Mind," by The Amboy Dukes, Ted Nugent's first band; or even "Spazz" by The Elastic Band; "Incense and Peppermints" by The Strawberry Alarm Clock.

What is this about time? How about "Strychnine" by The Sonics or "The Little Black Egg" by The Nightcrawlers? Maybe "Get Me to the World on Time" by The Electric Prunes or "Dirty Water" by The Standells.

We are back to eggs and the pink or green or blue plastic Easter egg hums on the kitchen table, ready for the Sunday service that will pop it open as it reveals its holy secrets.

The rock critic continues, "By any measure, the fabled tune's life path has been a remarkable one. This is a ditty that started life as the mere B-side of an R&B single, yet went on to bypass the Beatles' 'Yesterday' as the most frequently recorded rock song (currently about 1,600 versions) in history."

The man who walked down the street (no, his name isn't Louie) that Sunday was blessed because the war was on the other side of the world, though his family had been affected by the blind call, the young warriors of time and holidays racing to duty. Bless the warriors and the idea of democracy being planted in the ruins of the temple.

Someone paused and listened for the quiet guitars but they were put away months ago because electricity had been banned since everything ran on computers. Don't computers run on electricity? No, they are wireless and wireless is the way to go in the fresh century of invisible forces and candles and bread and old blankets and old rice and old sandals and old ideas and old feathers and old wishes and old love and old placements and old possessions and old freedom and old hatred and old liberty and old crosses and old rosaries and old faith and old white-washing and old brain-washing and old journeys because old thoughts and rebellion don't change anything because everyone is here in their belief. They simply add new songs to their iPods.

An underground whisper above the candle flame says, "Laser scanners with arrays of cameras can create digital 3-D models of objects that encode all the significant bumps, cracks, corners and facets of real things. Computers can enhance, morph or tweak the models before shipping them to 3-D 'printers' that may be halfway around the world."

This is why resurrection is the proven thing, why the long wait to go beyond fax machines may come to an end when the human body, along with its trapped soul, can be transported 3-D ripe and wind up somewhere else. No more cars, planes, or trains. Instant travel, though the soul is being screened by Homeland Security and the 3-D printer is not plugged in.

The whispering in the pews continued, "A man put his foot through a $300,000 painting Wednesday afternoon at the Milwaukee Art Museum and told museum workers later that the image disturbed him. Painted in 1640, the oil painting depicts the outcome of the biblical tale of David and Goliath, with David carrying the giant Goliath's severed head."
Milwaukee Journal Sentinel 04/05/07

A severed head? What about a loaf of bread to pass among the believers? A foot for art. A foot for history. A march toward artistic freedom. A way out of the sandals and into the Nike burners, all ideas forgotten, distaste for image sending the toes through the colors of time and memory.

Here we go again with time. Bring back that box set after you are done burning it onto your iTunes program.

On Easter Sunday, it is impossible to stop whispering: *"Variations: Selections from the Diane and Sandy Besser Collection features over 700 objects of art. From colorful beaded African crowns to finely carved Guatemalan slingshots, Variations features a dazzling collection of art from Asia, Africa and Latin America from the collection of Diane and Sandy Besser. Highlights include masks from Nepal, Mexico and Cameroon, sculpture, adornment, ceremonial and religious objects, and a variety of daggers and hilts from Indonesia."*

Slingshots and daggers are the passport and the collection collects money as thousands pour past the exhibit, the Guatemalan thing shown in honor of Christopher Columbus and what he had to go up against. What if someone wants to put his or her foot through the slingshot? Can it be done or will the independent soul, fresh out of candles, be hurtled across the jungle trees and into the 21ˢᵗ Century of RPDs and daggers?

He stood at the church door and suddenly recalled what the priest did to him as a child and he wanted to cry but reached for a finger dip of dirty holy water in the stone cup mounted on the wall. How many fingers were thrust in there on this Easter Sunday? How much blessed bacteria floats forgiven and chosen in that tiny pool of fuel?

The weeping man whispered, "A California company called Genetic Savings and Clone, Inc. was planning to offer cloned cats for sale; the company also hopes to clone dogs someday."

The old women kneeling on the hard concrete in front of the pews stopped their whispering and heard him and turned and watched him trip over a couple of worshippers as he searched for a place on the long benches. They were shocked because they knew this day was about resurrection and not about cloning.

The quiet guitars have not been forgotten, although the candle wax has formed an amazing psychedelic pattern on the kitchen table and, yes, that plastic egg is still there, though now it is spinning in a blur on the surface.

Miracles make good whispering, "It was reported that the human immune system produces ozone gas, and a large silo filled with biosolids, the popular fertilizer formerly known as sewage sludge, recently exploded in the Bronx."

Everyone knew the world ran on human time bombs. No more suicide car bombers. Throw shit. No, correction. Explode shit and be resurrected!

He filled himself with the wafer of confession and was free. He filled himself with the quiet guitar, though Robert Fripp, of King Crimson fame, cut a weird obscure solo album called Exposure in January 1979 and it is now a cult classic, freshly remastered and expanded to include every possible dimension of experimental and pure avant-soul rapture that means something only to those who have run out of candles and have too many places to plug in. Favorite tune on the amazing album— 'You Burn Me Up, I'm a Cigarette." Nothing about time? No, only the song "I May Not Have Enough of Me, But I've Had Enough of You."

This is not the blue window or the black cross or the yellow tide or the white whiskers or the green belly or the orange hair or the red horde or the brown skin. Are the basic colors used up on the computer screen? No, it is an Easter Blackberry with its battery highly charged. What about the pure pale vision of an Easter with colored plastic eggs, the chocolate candy inside their manufactured shells swallowed long ago, eaten before the communion wafer of situations?

Someone keeps whispering because they are tired of selling online tickets to the opening of the tomb, "Physicists in Romania recently created gaseous plasma blobs that grow, replicate themselves, and communicate, suggesting that life might emerge in unexpected circumstances."

He was correct all along. It is definitely about resurrection. The only problem is the thing about communication because, sooner or later, the world will run out of candles. In the end, it comes down to rock and roll, religion, and sex, with the whispering tongue licking the way, "Scientists have discovered the oldest known genitals, a very large penis on the fossil of a 400 million year old ancestor of the daddy longlegs spider."

To have faith, you must paint the symbol of a daddy longlegs on your quiet guitar and stop listening to so much electrified Miles Davis though, before he died, he had three heavy electric guitarists playing in one of his last bands. "Inamorata," "Sanctuary," "Masqualero," even "Blues for Pablo," though Pablo was resurrected a long time ago and the holidays can't be confused.

The whispering can only end when he finally finds a place among the kneeling, praying believers, makes the sign of the cross, takes off his iPod headphones, and blesses the Easter crowd with his last whisper, "It was reported that an elevator to outer space was under development and could be working in about fifteen years."

SET THE CONTROLS FOR THE HEART OF THE SUN

Set the controls for the heart of the sun, as the Pink Floyd song says, and you will be granted everything you have ever wished for. Of course, you have to do this inside your head because your body is going nowhere because it is planted in a field of sunflowers and you have been watching the army ants crawl over your protruding arms for years. This says the rest of your frame is stuck in the ground, shoved in there when the earth was alive and respected you one fine day by sticking you in the ground and leaving you to grow old alone, not to die, but to grow old staring at the thick stalks of sunflowers towering over your stinking, dirty, sweaty head.

Set the controls for the heart of the sun by claiming everything is okay as you move from sunflowers to magnificent collections of Gertrude Steins. These Gertrude Steins stand on their own two feet and release amazing words that line the path toward the sun you are heading for. These Gertrude Steins are expert pilots and they will handle the controls in amazing bursts of phrases, fragments, and sentences outlawed by the dinosaurs stuck back on the planet. If you claim everything by owning your very own collection of Gertrude Steins, you will begin to understand without having a single clue as to what is going on. You will find the endless verbal answer when your vehicle lands hard on the surface of the sun, thus smashing your fine Gertrude Steins into a million brilliant stars.

Set the controls for the heart of the sun before you realize your escape comes from the language embedded between your ears as if sunlight is both the cause and the cure, allowing your imagination to wonder if there is any water near the overhanging trees you spot in the distance as you carefully walk across a bright green field absent of sunflowers, though the high grass reminds you of your imprisonment that ended when you aimed at the burning ball up there and your desire to arrive came back as a sack of fresh lemons that landed in your arms, throwing you back on the grass, though you held onto the sack and only spilled one sharply yellow lemon that rolled in a direction that gave you one useful clue.

I Can't Help Myself

"If you cannot be seduced by beauty, you cannot learn the wisdom of ugliness." Hilda Dolittle

On windy days, I stand next to the dead. They speak to me, but I cannot understand the howling wind. It is a force of nature that has nothing to do with me.

When the volcano sleeps for centuries, no one is there to awaken the earth.

I was happy before I was told too many stories.

Beauty came and beauty went away before I could understand how it fit into the lives of great men who prospered and took the ugliness out of their hands.

Millions of people crossed the border into the desert, some living, some dying, some being killed by vigilante ranchers with blessed guns.

On the morning of historic change, she rested her chin on his shoulder.

On windy days, I come in, then go out and wonder what it takes to discover the sound of weeping, as if resistance is merely a dance swept away by a louder howling that shakes the windows and moves the doors.

How could the large man eat so many tortillas? Why did he suffer like he did—catching the many names they threw at him in the alley, some of the words later identified in a document the authorities found on his body, the missing names he was called before he died not making it onto the crumbled paper, disappearing in the history of loss, in the bible of grief, in the swirls of red chili he wiped up on his plate with the last shred of tortilla he ever ate.

There is no rain. It doesn't exist. It was banished from any idea of hope, dream, or vision. Even in this year of little snow, there was no such thing as rain because the falling water had gone too far, fallen too deeply into crevices in the earth no man would ponder. There is no rain. There is no reason to explain it. There is simply no water.

Raking leaves left-over from fall, getting the yard ready for spring, I wait for water and don't know where to look, how to dig and gather the yellow grass into mounds that will stay there until tomorrow. A gray spider darts up the fence and disappears. There is nothing else to see, nowhere to stand without getting in the way.

On windy days, I come inside the house and breathe deeply, stare at the bookshelf and wonder what happened to the book that taught me how to cross to the other side of the room.

Two days after no rain, it pours and cries and the storm does not cease for hours, the water running as if it heard me thinking about rain. It doesn't matter this does not have a meaning or an idea or a god or a way of being lost under the cross that was warped in the last flood. No one would listen or care, no one would stand in the rain and allow the raindrops to change the way they look, how they close their eyes each time the black sky reminds them there is a black sky.

To be anyone who will listen to you is a great challenge because the mute masters have taken over and the mountains vanished long ago because they could not tolerate the way you cried for them. Even the landscape lives and waits for your next move.

The guest was someone I loved, someone I hoped would love me in return before the empty corral reminded me the story of the western reaches ended in the last century and I was too late because I had already been born.

On windy days, equatorial bliss means there is a street where I have walked forty-two times and there is a lane where I have stepped twelve ways. There is also a boulevard I have never seen, but that remains clean and cobble-stoned on another planet.

She was lost and told her mother she was chased by a flying thing in the sky. Her mother believed her and loved her.

I came from the railroad worker who began as a young suffocated man in the sulfur mines of Yuma. When he died at the age of forty-one, I was not there, but I saw him fall and I traced the train tracks back to their source, the beginning where the rails point to the horizon and explode faster than the fastest man who tracks them toward the sun.

What does this have to do with confession? Why depend on the map?

They said dreams are not allowed. They told me not to talk about it. They warned me that the punishment for the dream would be so essential and deeply striking that I would never recognize myself again. I quit dreaming and went to sleep, instead.

When I started dreaming again, salamanders crept out of the right ear of my father and he finally acknowledged me.

When I swore I would not have any more nightmares, I kept having the recurring one I have had since I was a child—the long claw of someone pressing down on my wrists that are tied to the sacrificial stone table, my whole body strapped there as something historic is about to happen. Don't believe me. It is my recurring nightmare and I can't get rid of it.

The deer bounded through the trees and the white handkerchief fell in the grass.

A solid geometric word became the formula he was seeking and his arms fell at his sides and he realized the cube was tragic and composed of intricate circles without ownership or origin, yet their fate had been trapped in his rib cage for the entire length of his research fellowship.

Broken chambers integrate disputed amounts of earth without extracting elements of past conflict where diamond sandals were worn by the conquering muses that despised the mute fashion of the first poet who attempted to sing. His sliced-off head rolled only four feet away from the blossoming sacrifice no one documented because the world was flat.

I put the landscape in your face but you never noticed.

How the bass destroys the walls, how the amplifiers are candles.

It must be a mistake because I am dancing.

When the newspaper went up in smoke, I wasn't there, but the story was accurate and things changed and I had more money and was able to creep through the dark streets of the city with ease, my manuscripts well hidden, my secrets preserved, and the fame that obscurity never brings humming with victory behind the bricks of the church where I made my first confession as a ten-year-old boy.

Things fade, things go away, and the devil is but an imagined source of fire where the ones who believe are transformed into praying objects, not humans, but objects that sometimes tattoo a tiny cross on their foreheads, the black ash of yesterday pounding a thought or two about the road to high heaven where the relatives that made their lives miserable have been practicing a scorched earth policy since God took them up there.

I can't help it, but on windy days, I am handy with achievement.

JIMI IS WALKING

Jimi Hendrix is walking, moving towards the light, electric wires twisted around his head like a scarf bristling with fire from the place he is going. Jimi is walking, taking his time crossing the stage to bridge the smoke, carrying his quiet guitar in his arms.

Jimi is ascending toward the curtains, flames crackling over the mike because Jimi is walking closer to the amplifier where it happened. Jimi is plugging his heart into the machinery, the crowd screaming because Jimi is walking away from them.

Jimi is singing his song, the white guitar flashing through his heart because Jimi is walking and the tremendous feedback orders him to fly instead, the crowd growing larger, their faces on fire because Jimi is walking away from them, the electric chord slashing like a whip toward heaven.

SIX RISING PROSE POEMS

The beginning of the alphabet says we are supposed to stay hungry and not say a word. When this is true, checkered flowers grow on the foreheads of the ones we love. When this is false, we have nothing to say and are buried with our shoes on. The spoken tongue was forgotten when we grew up and learned to love computers. The buzzards circled without being able to plug into our memory banks. The spoken tongue became a religion we were trained not to question, only recite until faith was a fading monument to unhappy kings. This idea was taught to young boys until they earned their medals by bringing home startled, dead deer. This way of survival was taught to young girls until they kept the house clean of spiders, worms, and fingerprints from strangers who visited when the boys were away reloading their guns.

*

A man and a woman exchange phone numbers but never call each other because they each meet someone else, the pieces of paper with those numbers staying in their possession. One day, four years after their meeting at a party, the man finds the note with the woman's name. He dials the number and an old priest at one of the largest churches in the city answers in a sleepy voice. When the man asks for the woman on the slip, the priest hesitates, then says, "She died four years ago."

*

A man and a man exchange wallets and get away with it. They are enemies but do not know it because their driver's licenses do not show a trace of their past history, how they organized groups of men to enter the night streets and cause harm, wearing different colored uniforms to tell each other apart. A man and a man exchange wallets and never explain to anyone why they would do such a thing, this act committed before the greater powers slap handcuffs on both and lead them into the heart of the machine where bodies of earlier men lay as skeletal sculptures, as murals, the white bones dwarfed by huge mountains of brown and black wallets piled against sweating walls.

*

A woman and a boy were mother and child and were forgiven by the husband and father. He had to forgive them in order to keep his sanity, his blue socks frozen to his thin, pale legs, his tired body coming home from selling used cars until late at night, his tired breathing leading him to the unmade bed where he fell every night, his silence and wisdom hanging in the night air for the woman and boy to stare at when they stood in the doorway and wondered if it was safe to call out his name.

*

The road was painted purple and railroad engineer caps hung from the trees. I knew the barrio was a golden opportunity, so I could not believe what I saw. The peppermint ice cream cone cost three cents. The orchard was washed in silver shade and the trees produced Christmas ornaments sold at Halloween. I pulled the beetle out of my arm and laughed at its sting. My shoelaces were green, the sneakers orange, and the socks light blue. The arch over the road was made of branches stripped of their railroad engineer caps. I assumed the rusting cars in the woods had dead bodies rotting inside. When I approached the first one, a football came flying out of it, but I missed the catch and it bounced into the stream. The fence surrounded the entire world and the purple road was no longer that color, but a deep, fleshy line toward someone's beating heart. I wanted the striped candy, but got the onion flavored chewing gum instead. At the road's end, there was a house made of baby diapers sewn together, fresh, clean material untouched by baby life, the white walls of this house waiting for someone to admit "This is a house made of baby diapers."

*

He stopped on the corner and saw his lover float by as a naked angel, her wings waving to him as she passed him several feet off the ground, the baby blue dress she wore something he recalled from the first day they met. He looked both ways and started to cross the empty street when a fast car came skidding around the corner, followed by a police car with red lights, no siren. He was caught in the middle of the street and his angel reached down and plucked him from harm, the bad and good guys speeding by too fast to notice he hung on in terror as his angel lover whisked him into the clouds. As they flew toward heaven, his

62

life was real, her life done, but his memories of a broken heart were intact miles above the earth, making no difference in how he felt or lived. Suddenly, his lovely angel changed her mind and let go of his hand.

Profit from Reality

As in your twenty-one-year-old nephew making it out alive after two tours of duty in Iraq. As in the sprained tendon in your right foot you hurt while running on a treadmill. Cash in like the shadow chasing the tiger out of the books, the waterfall reaching for the heart and changing it into a tractor pulling a flying saucer out of the mud, its aliens dead inside, the government vaults corroded with lies, the actual truth profiting from being left alone as in the two-headed farmer mutating in the barn, the wheat he grew livid with purple and orange stalks glowing on his birthday, the farm isolated and out of reach, his plight reaching you through cyber spies searching for the last toilet roll in Elvis' bathroom where he died.

Profit from this atmosphere as in your nephew's attitude about going back to Iraq as an armed civilian contractor if he can't find a job at home, this urge to return to the interior the same as the germinating pebbles in your brain, their existence the cause of an elegance you display each time someone hands you an invitation to the dance and you never go, turning them down with the excuse your remarkable predator is pacing on the ocean floor and you have to be ready to get rich when the beast rises to the surface and tries to cash in on his legend by making you a hero from the word "Go!"

No Knowledge

No knowledge without the secrets of how the caraganda grew into a hairy shape that inflicted harm by weaving a solid invasion without having to grow the ears of Saint Ignatius who was slain, his head cut off and his body picking it up off the ground and walking with it under his arms, dropping it on the spot where he wanted to be buried.

This implies there are engines buzzing inside holy ghosts, wheels building new roads to protect old roads, paths coming back when the fire ants take over the yard, burning themselves into a black stream like the vein that kept Saint Ignatius alive with fresh, stinging ideas.

He put his head back on and insisted someone tell him why the books are always open to the right page, why his head became a turtle in the grass that grew without hesitation and fit properly back on his shoulders.

When a young boy tripped and fell down a mountainside, his broken soul regained form, the pain and awareness forming a blood rose in his brain, the sleep he endured at the bottom of the mountain bringing him humiliation, along with a strong horse. He rose after the coma and was seen as a tall, eroding statue of a nameless god that angered the invaders, though it was allowed to be propped in the village square. The town built a church around his chest, roads around his knees, and a whorehouse around his head, the statue the last place where widows stopped and wept.

The boy inside the stone never awoke and is an artifact to this day, even after seven earthquakes took the invaders away. There is no knowledge without open equations satisfying the distance between the sextant and Saint Ignatius' head. Even the reason for placing his ignorance in the correct sentence gives this history a fresh turn, the idea that will swim toward apprenticeship and the start of a punctual edge in the boy's trapped heart.

THINGS YOU DON'T SEE ANYMORE

A unicorn taking a dump on the street corner or two wrinkled hands dipped in cooking flour suddenly turning into the two hands of the one with the explosive belt and the one way ticket to martyrdom. The first pair of shoes you wore as a baby or the first cow tongue your mother cooked when you were four years old, the smell fumigating the house.

A thousand cabbages raining down from the sky onto a busy city street or a man spreading venom from the rattlesnake he killed yesterday onto his breakfast toast. The last cricket your cat ate or the very first car, an old VW bug, your father bought you in high school, even the last ashes the priest smeared on your forehead on the last Ash Wednesday you went to church thirty years ago.

A teacher with a bout of diarrhea running out of the classroom or a fugitive escaping through the bathroom window as the teacher runs in. The longest worm crawling out of the tomato or a butterfly infestation in the backyard during the harshest winter in twelve years, the white butterflies fluttering out of the snow drifts. A unicorn circling the bare tree in late summer, its silver flanks glistening in the hot sun as a little girl stands against the tree and closes her eyes.

The pair of deer antlers you found stuck high in a tree years ago, the trail into that wilderness that became overgrown with tall grass the following autumn when you made a second visit to climb the tree and extract the horns, but the horns were gone.

ON A VISIT TO SAN FRANCISCO

Three men on a pier were planning an attack on themselves. I watched them as distant ships passed beyond the cold harbor. The men paced back and forth, seagulls mocking their secrecy. Kenneth Rexroth awoke from the dead and walked the same pier. He shook his head, daring me in silence to quote a line or two from his words.

The white horizon could not respond to the old poet as he buttoned his coat and strolled away. When the fog came in, I waited for the boat, but someone said the boat stopped over there. When I walked in the fog, something hit the water to my right, perhaps a flying fish taunting the waves. I crossed the pier and sat in a café with coffee, Rexroth leaning on a lamp post outside, his white hair moving in the wind, his eyes closed.

I climbed the paved hills and struggled up North Beach, until I came to a door, an opening where men argued, drinking away the prison and the shame, bowing to asphalt and saying poems—"This is the street where we scratch our names on pavements that hold up the walls." I studied the bricks that parted the fog, but could not read the names, the white chalk of the dead reciting obscure passages and twisted hopes, dreams where Kerouac lights a candle and spills a glass.

I tried to honor the bricks, but the walls held. I drank my coffee and listened to men who insisted the walls were there and I was not strong enough to go through the corridors of speech, the silence we are granted because what we want to say is already burned up there. I finished my coffee in the empty place, but Rexroth never came in. I left, slipped down a back alley to smell Chinese food, a turning in the air before a pair of dark shoulders, leaning against bricks, pointed—"No, that way."

Room Thirteen

In room thirteen, the wooden stairs from the old whorehouse are stored, lying on their side like an enormous accordion that won't close. There is ancient air and darkness that have not seen an open door, or felt human presence, in forty-two years. In that same room, three untapped kegs sit, the brew inside having turned to solid gold. In room thirteen, there is one window, but it can't be reached. It is up in the top left corner, a small diamond shape letting small bits of light inside. In the room, there are two narrow bunk beds, the mattresses long gone, the wire springs rusting with age. Room thirteen is full of doubt, but it can't be felt, though things can be seen in there if anyone can find the door and make it past the four locks. The room contains an old trunk that has not been opened in forty-two years, the dust on top of the trunk as thick as the ancient curtains hanging over the closet that has no door. It is unknown what lies or hangs in the closet because the decaying curtains are too thick.

Room thirteen will catch fire someday and be the origin of a conflagration that will burn down the entire structure, though the form, shape, and size of the structure has nothing to do with the room. In the meantime, there are stationary things in the room that want to move a few inches, but are blocked by an enormous dresser whose drawers are empty except for the top one that sits open halfway. Inside it is a toothbrush and a small black-and-white photograph of an old four-story house, though it is not the structure that holds room thirteen. In the room, something moves slightly, but goes unseen. In the room, something else wants to move, but never will.

WANDERING PACKS OF GODS

The god of condoms wandered the world and gave millions of packs away. The god of disease flew across the planet and planted wherever he could, his secret spores dug up by the god of x-ray vision, this god in conflict with the god of vacuum cleaners who was supposed to follow behind and make sure all plague was sucked up. The god of nuclear power was hidden in a concrete vault, while the god of sunlight bathed nude next to the god of sand who was sunbathing after the god of the sea drowned earlier in the day, the huge wave that took him formed by the god of islands who grew tired of all the water surrounding his kingdom, so he puffed and turned the currents back toward the continent where the god of the desert roamed beyond the mountains in search of the god of ice cream who was melting at the foot of the god of bisexuality who lay at the foot of the first mountain carved by the god of carnal doubt. The god of eyeglasses appeared out of nowhere and stared at the wandering packs of gods who roamed the planet and decided they all needed new pairs of shades, so they would stop doing what they were doing on earth and return to heaven without going blind. Before he could distribute new sunglasses to the pack, the god of scissors appeared and sheared off the long hair of the god of eyeglasses. This made him go blind and he fell into a canyon where the god of exile was hiding, his wings comfortably folded over the god of libraries who was reading a book while his partner slept. The blind god didn't notice them, so he crawled away, until he fell through a crevice in the canyon and rolled to stop before the god of "What the hell?"

PART 3

THE GUITARS

When Bob Dylan unstrapped his acoustic guitar after recording a few songs for *Blood on the Tracks*, he forgot the two other songs he had been carrying in his head. When he picked up the guitar in the studio again, he wrote a different song that never made it on the record, though the two forgotten songs appeared on bootlegs. The last guitar John Lennon played before he was murdered stood against the cold fireplace in his New York apartment, the leather collar he wore on the cover of *Two Virgins* tied around the neck of the guitar. When Eric Clapton's four-year-old son fell out of a 49th floor apartment to his death, there were two electric and two acoustic guitars in the room with the open window.

The guitar Pete Townshend smashed at Monterey in 1967 was salvaged for parts in a London shop, the instrument shipped back in pieces from California. The guitar Jimi Hendrix burned at Monterey was never seen again after the show, his roadies claiming for years that it simply vanished backstage. When Patti Smith performed her last concert before her husband Fred suddenly died, the guitar she played that night was a pure white Stratocaster. After the last gig Mick Abrahams played with Jethro Tull, he sold four of his guitars and did not play any for two years. The last time Jimmy Page used a violin bow on his Les Paul, the friction between the bow and the guitar strings disintegrated the bow halfway through the song.

Two days before blowing himself away, Kurt Cobain threw seven electric guitars he owned into the street outside his Seattle home, keeping five acoustic guitars in the last bedroom where he slept. Lou Reed found a guitar in his coat closet he had not seen in years, the red instrument leaning against the back of the closet, a black t-shirt draped over it. Joni Mitchell lost two dark purple guitar picks on stage the last time she played a song from *Blue,* signaling a roadie for another after the two picks flew from her strumming fingers into the audience. Before taking the outdoor stage in Mexico City, in front of a crowd of 80,000, Carlos Santana knelt before three unplugged electric guitars, rubbed herbal oil up and down the frets, wiped the moisture with a cloth, then stuck three rosary beads in the guitars, one bead per instrument embedded in a tiny hole he had someone drill in each solid body. When the first print for the cover of George Harrison's *All Things Must Pass* was developed, it showed a guitar lying in the grass near the elves surrounding George. He swore there was no guitar and the photo was reshot, the second showing the elves without the guitar. A biographer of The Beatles later claimed Harrison told him the first photo contained one of the first guitars he played in the group, an instrument he sold years before leaving the band and recording his first solo album. The guitar photo is somewhere in the Harrison archives.

Joe Strummer used the same acoustic guitar on his three Mescalero albums, his last work before dying. The last time Neil Young played "Like a Hurricane" in concert, his rare black Les Paul produced feedback that burned a dark line across the forehead of a fan who was leaning on the stage in front of Neil. She never knew where it came from and couldn't wash it off. Her doctor told her it could lead to skin cancer and she needed to stay away from tanning beds. An unknown Tommy Bolin was sixteen years old when he jumped onstage barefoot at a Grateful Dead concert in Denver, jamming with the band on several songs. Two days later, someone broke into his Boulder apartment and stole his only guitar, the young musician having less than ten years to live.

Peter Green had a nervous breakdown halfway into Fleetwood Mac's 1968 tour of the U.S. The day it happened, he awoke in a New York hotel to find each of his three guitars had one broken string. He spent the day restringing them and screaming at roadies, until everyone left him alone in his room. When he didn't show up for the sound check, the crew found an empty room and several guitar strings bristling on the floor. Jerry Garcia dreamed about his cut-off finger only twice in his life. The first time was on his thirty-fifth birthday, which was a day he took four acid tabs. The second dream came years later, the night after the Dead played a forty-five minute version of "Dark Star" and Jerry switched guitars half an hour into the song. The second dream was of a white guitar with silhouettes of his finger tattooed all over the shiny instrument.

One day after quitting The Yardbirds, Jeff Beck plugged his Les Paul into brand new Marshall amps and blew them out without playing a note.

When he pulled the plug, a blue spark shot up his right hand. Frank Zappa fired off a fiery solo in the middle of "Black Napkins," his bare chest covered in sweat, his tight bell-bottom trousers now soaked, his feet moving across the stage in huge platform shoes, the crowd teasing Frank, a girl throwing paper flowers. Frank grabbed a pink rose in mid-air and stuffed it between the many dials and buttons on his guitar, the ridiculous act of a fan throwing paper flowers making Frank turn his back to the audience as he let out a tremendous fart no one heard under the heavy wall of sound his band was laying down. Duane Allman saw the truck cross his path the instant before his motorcycle slammed into it, the bright flash forming his last thought which was the realization he had two dark purple guitar picks in his jacket pocket.

Emmylou Harris strummed her guitar in the overpowering lights of the tiny club, her first public performance of "Boulder to Birmingham," a song about Gram Parsons, taking place before an audience of sixty people, fourteen of them guitar players. Five years earlier, Keith Richards lent a strung-out Gram a guitar so he could sit in on the *Exile on Main Street* sessions. Gram's contributions to several songs were erased by The Stones, though Keith stole a great guitar solo from Gram and used it on a later song. The last time Gram played live on stage, he noticed how many people were lighting cigarettes in the dark club, the tiny flames of their lighters flickering across the room and reflecting on the smooth body of his brand new guitar.

UNACKNOWLEDGED

It is a kite on fire up high over the sandy beach, a propeller tracing smoke across the void in the ear of a clown tired of his nightly performance before smelly crowds, three pairs of handkerchiefs with the DNA of a beheaded saint, the faint aura of existence crowding his executed shadow until it forms flowers that grow out of the mud walls of the temple. Perhaps the Volvo speeding away after the hit and run, or a tiny macho beetle climbing into the ear of the priest, twelve black widow spiders coming to life under the old wooden platform he sat on inside the shadows of the confessional, even a learned alphabet corrupting the orphan lost on the street, though the shiny beetle in the ear of the priest cannot be comprehended because it is on a different path and to go in that painful, bleeding direction would change the canon and realign the text he depends on each morning, noon, and night, his awareness that his hearing will finally accept the sound of angelic wings.

It was actually a kite painted in bright flames spinning high above the crashing waves. An apron from the last grandmother fell in the laundry room still smelling of tortillas, though the word "tortilla" has been outlawed since three caterpillars were found in the *masa* and one of them contained the formula for Venus and Jupiter, the crushed body of one caterpillar turning the tortillas green but, again, the word becomes *rapodolores* as in Dolores, the ancient girl who whispered into the ear of Cortez and convinced him the New World was worth destroying. It was truly a kite in smoke, guided by the expert hands of a young girl who refused the idea that her mother was to blame for the conquest.

The sudden bed spring and the sugar free can of awful tasting Coke. The biological relationship between an eggplant and a tobacco leaf because both contain nicotine, though the purple lips of the eggplant eater are not related to the black lips of the smoker. Actually the broken twig, a shirt that fits, three cases of CDs no one plays any longer because all their music is on the computer. Don't forget three ink pens and one useless pencil, even the taste of oranges wrapped in oily buffalo leaves tied into knots that resemble a tiny man's face, the tight ball of fiber slowly rotting until the knots transform into the profile of the surviving nun,

the one who got away and was able to convince the historians there is
no responsibility for conquest unless you are able to catch at least one
of the black widow spiders from the darkness of the confessional and
swallow it whole, the reaction causing the invisible soul who performed
the act to have his face printed on the burning kite as it completes loop
after loop in the air before falling straight to the hard sand, disintegrat-
ing into thousands of pieces.

NOT AGAIN

The feral hog population in East Texas is out of control, wildlife scientists warned, and one rancher said he was afraid to let his grandchildren leave the yard. When I read that, I was afraid and would not leave my yard, though I don't live in East Texas. I admit I am a native of the state, but all I saw were the mounted heads of javelinas on walls belonging to some of my childhood friends' fathers, wild boars with their sharp tusks curved toward ceilings I could never reach.

Dutch surgeons implanted tiny pieces of jewelry in the eyes of six women and one man. I implanted tiny pieces of glass in my left eye and it made me see farther, the red blur becoming white as I stared at rich people stumbling toward me.

Astrophysicists suggested that a highway of dark matter ripped from the dwarf galaxy Sagittarius, which is being consumed by the Milky Way, is streaming right through Earth. I felt this plunging stream when I stood on the green grass of my backyard, shut my eyes, and spread my arms wide. Several dwarfs jumped out of the evergreens and knocked me down. As my face skidded across the slippery grass, I felt the stream go through me. When I opened my eyes, the earth had changed, the dwarfs had gone back to their galaxy and I needed to go to the bathroom.

Scientists in California successfully implanted a brain prosthesis in a dish of rat brain slices, and a similar array of rat brain cells was able to fly a virtual F-22 fighter jet. When I ducked, the jet crashed into a mountain in a ball of flame and that was the end of the rat Air Force. Of course, this proves that a militaristic genetic code exists inside the rat and answers many questions I have about the violent, shrinking world and how the idea of "rat" and rat conquest begins in the soul.

It was reported that wild elephants, often drunk on rice beer, were terrorizing several villages in India. When one spinning elephant was shot by a hired hunter, it threw up several gallons as it fell to its enormous knees and died. The beer-barf explosion set off a tsunami that washed away all the rice beer for two hundred miles, the heavy bile drowning twenty of the alcoholic elephants who were either too drunk or hung-over to run. The lesson learned is that a lone, reeling elephant should not be shot when it is drunk. It is that simple. No mystery, no puzzle, no joke. A drunk, tottering elephant should not be shot.

A new study found that the children of older fathers have a greater risk of going crazy later in life. This proves that the longer you wait to create a family, the harder it is to stay out of the nut house, yet this also says that delaying the act of extending the family line gives the older father more time to mess up his life. When he finally impregnates his 23 year-old wife at the ripe age of 57, he forms a condition known as "swift knee," as in knee to the groin, knee to the eye, and knee to the head. What this has to do with the forthcoming insanity of his children is not clear, though a study is underway to determine if the cure is making sure that certain mothers are at least 50 years of age before they have their first child.

ANSWER THE PETROGLYPH

If you could answer the petroglyph, the palm of your hand would be drawn on the wall. If you could repeat the sound, you would not stand there, but hide. If you could avoid going back to the patterns, you would leave the buried earth and turn your attention to the crawling lines on the forehead of a living sign, the forsaken mark drawn by the blue vein that did not mount the wall to be preserved as an undecipherable moment of a private life, its dangerous dimensions rewriting the text before your face.

If you could question the petroglyph, the palms of your eyes would be excused from their blindness, the image becoming the pattern of hope where your attempts to make sense out of historic damage are simply acts that hold back the crumbling surface, the markings being there to announce a silence that will eat your insides because the ancient squares and diamond shapes were incorrectly identified as triangles and circles.

If you could redraw the petroglyph, the interference would crack the surface and allow the art to be preserved under glass, this crime changing the uses of your toes in a disasterous century where the vanishing point of what you lack is actually a stone worm coming out of the wall next to the symbols, crawling down the wall toward your feet in the sand.

Anti Aphorism

He who makes his fingers walk does not know the path.

He who blinks one eye has wisdom.

He who blinks two eyes could be the bastard dropping out of the cage.

He who swallows the banana whole is the one who knows hunger.

He who stands under the moose could be the dynamite used to blow the bridge.

He who stares into the mirror is the one left behind.

He who mounts the widow from behind is told to hurry.

He who mounts the widow from the front tells her to hurry.

He who waits for a rainbow lives in the wrong century.

He who insists there are three arms on his body is destined for greatness.

He who blows the whistle is bending in the direction of the widow.

He who loves the pear gave up the peach.

He who paints a single diamond on a sheet of paper forgets the theory of art.

He who walks with one untied shoe knows the path.

He who walks with two untied shoes cut the path.

He who bends the spines of books is destined to read secret stories.

He who reads books wearing white gloves is the author of a classic text.

He who recalls the sidewalk marked with chalk from childhood is stuck in time.

He who white-washes the sidewalk is the keeper of territories.

He who whispers on the street corner down from the sidewalk makes history.

He who believes in history has no shadow.

THE MINNESOTA LEG

The Minnesota leg stuck out of the snow for two days after the blizzard before I went to look. I crossed the street in front of my house and stopped before the huge snow bank. The leg protruded straight up, the shoe missing, one athletic sock in the cold like a flag marking the spot where one of my neighbors could have been hit by a snow plow. It reminded me of that scene in *Fargo* where the bad guy is grinding his late buddy into hamburger, his socked foot sticking out of the wood chipper. No one else was around the empty lot between houses. I grabbed the Minnesota leg with my gloved hands and pulled. The sock was frozen to the foot and I slipped and fell on my ass in the snow.

The leg flew through the air and plopped in the snow, a red string tied at the point right below the knee where the leg was probably dismembered from some fool's body. I got to my knees and grabbed the string. At the end of it, wrapped in a sandwich bag to keep the moisture out, was a note that read "Quit pulling my leg." I dropped the thing and managed to get to my feet as the deep roar of a snow plow came around the corner. I moved out of the way and the truck threw a heavy wall of snow against me, knocking me down with the fresh taste of dirty snow covering my mouth. The driver didn't slow down or act like he saw me as he rumbled up the street doing his job. I wiped the snow out of my eyes and off my wool cap. Part of the red string stuck out of the snow. I reached for it and found it was no longer attached to the Minnesota leg. As I stared at the wet string, I heard another motor approaching and thought it was another plow, but this sound was more shrill.

A kid flew by on his smoking snow mobile. He turned to look at me as the stinking fumes from his machine left a trail behind him. Before I could lift my heavy, snow covered boots and try to get home, the kid's German Shepard leaped out of nowhere, the Minnesota leg in its jaws. The dog growled as it passed me, the bare foot missing its sock, the toes turning blue as if they were alive. The dog hopped crazily through the snow pack, the leg dangling in its mouth. I looked both ways and made it to my side of the street. Before shaking the last of the snow off my coat, I spotted the white sock frozen to the bare branches of the evergreen tree in my front yard.

Retrieval

An Apache chief stares into the camera three days before he is killed. Your empty palm rises in the air, the door creaking, your aging body asking for elegance. This opening is forgotten when light descends to cut the frame for the door—the invention of churches forgiven after the door is closed. If you get there, your fingers trace the postcard of the Apache taped on your mirror, a surge of sparrows ascending in patterns impossible to read.

Don't hold the photo for one hundred years.

Fingerprints on the ivory doorknob are left by a spirit hovering in the doorway. These are choices from the night before. One is a Kachina doll wrapped in a box, its arms broken off, the bringer of gifts not knowing the difference between giving and reaching out. The second is the forest floor—sun, some leaves, the crackling underfoot making you stop, your camera focusing on a running figure found in your archival papers one hundred years from now.

FINDINGS (3)

New research suggests that pointing enhances understanding. In some cultures, pointing is a faux pas, sometimes even insulting. New research is turning the social don't on its head, showing that hand gestures, such as pointing, can enhance the understanding of messages and make sex more pleasurable—the pointing having to extend at the right moment. An Alaskan scientist found that grizzly bears, during the spring season, spin in a tight circle right before charging their prey. He found the bears charge head on, without spinning, during winter. A woman who swallowed three penny coins swears they came out as nickels at the other end. A psychiatrist who examined her found a quarter under her tongue.

Scientists in Austin, Texas took a skunk and fed it nothing but cornmeal for three weeks. After that time, they found the sac of offensive musk had completely dried and the skunk was unable to spray. A robot, exploring a narrow cave in New Mexico, lost all power and contact with the technicians on the surface as soon as it stopped next to an ancient clay jar lying in the cave. They were unable to recover it forty feet below the desert. It was discovered that circumcised men are six to eight times less likely to have intercourse in the missionary position. Mexican surgeons removed three dead baby alligators from the stomach cavity of a bull that escaped from a ranch in northern Mexico, then was found dead a few miles away. The surgeons were puzzled because alligators are not native to the area.

NASA scientists concluded that the total number of satellites of unknown origin they are now tracking stands at 2,856. A new study concluded that eating raw onions raises the heart rate in men, but lowers it in women. Internet investigators have been able to keep track of a larger number of individuals downloading illegal music with new software that interprets the warmth given off by hands on the keyboard, which sets off magnetic sensors under the keyboard letters directly tied to the program. A Pennsylvania biologist uncovered the code that makes saliva in the mouth turn to cooking oil. American scientists announced they will no longer accept research samples of dinosaur egg fossils from countries outside the U.S. They refused to state a reason for banning them.

Researchers found that repeated exposure to low-level magnetic fields, such as those emitted by vibrators and VCRs, lead to a higher rate of prostate cancer in men.

The Floating House

You are inside the floating house and joy prospers in every corner.
Someone prays in the house while you are there and you are concerned
that the prayer could tip the balance and the house no longer float. It
is also a place for lost things, so the chanting that grows louder as you
ride your floating house has to be allowed. You stay inside your room
and decide everything is okay because the sound has died down and
your house is now passing beautiful waterfalls and sites of ancient bat-
tles where owners of castles and caves once dwelled. When your house
comes to the wonderful cliffs of paradise, it goes over and hurtles down
toward the things you used to ignore. When your floating house ex-
plodes on the rocks below, you are spared because you were kneeling in
the closet, trying on a pair of old socks you found when you crawled in
there, the smelly things reminding you there are things in your floating
house you refuse to do.

WILLOW

There is a willow growing in the back yard. Near its trunk is a statue of a gargoyle perched on a rock. Mud and a few blades of grass cover part of the gargoyle's clawed feet. Water from the hose seeps down the hill and into the bed of mulch surrounding the willow, creating a pool of water around the gargoyle.

Once there was a farm located on the property where the house with the willow was built. The farmhouse burned down twelve years before the property was sold and became part of a new housing development that eventually brought a young willow to be planted there.

The first light bulb in the neighborhood burned out in a basement room in the first house built on the newest section of lots the city allowed.

There is a tiny black mole that digs tunnels in parts of the backyard garden near the willow. The slippery animal was spotted once by the owner of the house, but the mole disappeared under some rocks.

Once there were three willows growing on the other side of a castle wall, but how they got there is a mystery because ancient times did not call for tracking the growth of those trees, though they can be found in an etching of a rare manuscript in the library where the woman, who lives in the house that has a willow growing in the backyard, works.

The killdeer built her nest in the grass a few yards from the willow and laid three blue eggs there.

There is the person who sculpted the gargoyle, but he lives in California and doesn't pay attention to willow trees.

When the locusts arrive, with everyone notified through advance news stories and internet warnings, they eat everything in sight but leave the willow alone, though the statue of the gargoyle bristles with dozens of locusts that have alighted upon it. The owners suffer over their destroyed garden, dead sod, and numerous plants and bushes killed by the locust infestation.

The entire property is redone and replanted at a cost of several thousand dollars as the willow continues to grow taller and thicker, now covering much of the devastated yard.

One year after the invasion of the locusts, the woman who works in the library looks out her window at the willow and notices the gargoyle is gone. This brings a flashback to her childhood home, where her parents planted a young willow tree in their front yard that was removed a few years later when they divorced.

The woman goes to the gardening center where she bought the first gargoyle and buys two more she places under the large willow tree in her backyard.

THE LAST MAYAN INDIAN

He stands silently on the street corner as cars go by. Some people wave to him when they recognize him as the last Mayan Indian. Mayans believe in fire clouds. When the world burns, those that are caught standing on busy street corners in major American cities are forgiven and brought back to their people. This last Mayan waves down my cab and hops in.

I don't know what I am doing picking up someone who looks like him. I turn over my right shoulder and greet him, but he just stares straight ahead. "Where to?" I ask as I head into heavy traffic. He doesn't answer, so I reach the red light on the corner and stop. "Where to?" I turn to him in a growing panic.

I have never had a passenger skip out on a fare, or jump into my cab without saying a word. The last Mayan blinks once, buttons his long trench coat and suddenly jumps out of my cab. "Hey!" I yell, but it is too late, and he has only ridden half a block.

Mayans believe that if you touch your sweating chest with a burning ember, you will be able to walk across any bridge and enter the green world with a new face, a pure soul, and be the ruler of your enemies.

I drive home thinking about my brief encounter with the last Mayan Indian. I am very tired and go to sleep when I get into my apartment. I don't even notice the tiny black cross smeared on my forehead. The ashes have not yet started to turn moist and run down my sleepy face.

Pattern Recognition

The old Indian woman with no legs pushing herself on the wheeled plat-form that gets her around. The hand opening with one solitary black rosary bead in the palm. An ill old man sitting up in the hospital bed, another old man sitting up behind him, a third old man sitting behind the second, a fourth rising, a fifth. Daisies blooming in a garden absent of bees. One hand on the forehead, tracing the wrinkles across the skin. Two words repeated in a hallway decades ago, echoing back to be said again, the person speaking recognizing what the words mean. Ancient sea shell crushed upon ancient sea shell next to the broken clay mask embedded between flat stones inside the rock chamber fallen beneath pyramid stairs blocking the path to revelation and understanding. A small boy running up the street, his wide open mouth locked in a silent scream, his arms outstretched to the sky, something trailing behind him. A domestic cat ripping the sides of a sofa with its claws, the mate-rial unraveling slowly over time.

The old Indian woman with no legs pushing herself across a busy in-tersection, the traffic stopping to let her roll herself to the other side of the street. Burned toast popping up in the toaster, the thin smoke trailing toward the fan above the stove. Fingerprints under the micro-scope identified as belonging to the person they have been looking for. A handwritten note with no name on it. A handwritten love note with two names on it. The buttons in the system ready to be pushed, the key-board in tune with the countdown, the lights and screens blinking where they should, the code given as accurate as possible, the software glitch waiting for the right moment. Directions followed on a map printed off a computer program. No one saying what it is. No one wanting to say what it is. No one wanting to speculate on what it might be. No one will-ing to announce what they know, in their hearts, it really is. The old In-dian woman with no legs on her wooden platform with wheels, waiting for a handout as a crowd of well-dressed people pours out of an enor-mous cathedral after Sunday services.

THE MUD MAN

The mud man came out of the Rio Grande the night before my grandfather died. He was a secret thought in the village—a mud man covered in the slime of slaves. Body of brown crosses and startled hair. Body of stinking clay and dark leaves in the eyes.

The mud man danced on the far bank of the river, cottonwood limbs moving above his head. He was blind and crusted in the brain. Unable to talk, he wandered the upper valley, frightened the crows and lit fires with his feet. In one house, my grandfather lay dying, the smell of approaching mud keeping him alive.

When the candles around his bed went out, he raised one hand and pointed to the door. My grandmother opened it in silence. The mud man stood there dripping his life. When the mud man approached, my grandfather closed his eyes. The last thing my grandmother recalled was her husband's dirt mask coming off, the bright streaks of mud across his face showing her what he looked like as a boy.

The mud man flew through the window as my grandmother shouted a curse. When other family members ran into the room, her husband was dead. When they saw the mud, they said a prayer.

When the river floods, there is no mud man. When the river dries, the mud man might come, but no one has seen him since the death of my grandfather and no one says anything about the mud on the shoes of every man who postpones his death.

CANTO

Under the leaves, the kiss of the snail. Hidden in the bricks, the whisper of spider webs spelling what went away. All things pray in the silence madness brings. You are recognized in the bringing when your father returns in a dream, his shoulder-blade shields repelling love. He worked too hard, sweated in rivulets that left marks on a man, his ladder to the sky a sculpture from his labor. You have not said anything about the puzzle of two rivers, one tree, and twenty sad people who knew him. Under their photos, the touch of skin. Somebody suddenly shouts, "The world ended yesterday. What are you doing here?"

They hope your answer arrives on time. How often do you count your toes before going to sleep? The great rooms are beautiful. You will re-member them when it is time for a new house—walls of embers flying to tell us what you missed because the stars are tired of being written about. Many things are true when it is difficult to love the other, so stand on the earthly side. Walk against the road and listen to the crows call you, chords vibrating inside conch shells of living blood. Remove your hat because prophetic dreams are going to show pity on the bou-levards. They will become streets of tenderness, until what follows you leaves stubborn scars on your arms.

PARAGRAPH PROTECTION

When he wrote it down, it disappeared before his eyes, so he had to write it again from memory. He stared at the paragraph in his trusty notebook in fear the ink would disappear again. He sat at his desk and waited. Minutes went by and the green ink stayed on the page. He stared at the paragraph and wondered how he could protect it from the world. Then, as he thought more about it, he wondered how he could protect his fresh block of text from himself, though he was pleased and impressed he had remembered every single word of the original paragraph. It only took seconds for him to feel normal after the brief scare of having his writing vanish before his eyes. Maybe it was the paper.

He set his favorite pen down and felt unsure. He should have written it down in his usual black ink, though he always knew when to reach for the special green pen. This happened about once or twice a month, a page or two of green paragraphs appearing among pages of black. He stopped speculating on colors of ink and stared at his words. They were still there, returning through fresh insight, the magical act of creation making him write the paragraph down in the first place. He wanted to overlook the fact they were the first green sentences that had momentarily vanished from his notebook. He wasn't blind and always wore eyeglasses. He had to continue so a disappearing paragraph would happen again. He picked up the green pen in his right hand and leaned over the page. He started to read, but the words he had written started changing before his eyes. The scrambling green letters of his tiny handwriting style made it difficult to see what new words were replacing the old. He rubbed his eyes with one hand, almost lost his eyeglasses off his nose, and jumped back when he saw what his paragraph had become.

It was the handwriting of someone else, though it belonged to him. When he realized what this meant, he panicked because he didn't know how to protect what he had written. He hurried to the window of his study and looked out at the cold winter morning. It had snowed the night before and the dim glow of white on the ground had given him the idea for the paragraph he wrote. He stared out the window until he found what he was looking for—small rabbit tracks weaving across the snow. He went back to his desk, sat down, and saw the paragraph had stopped changing. He read the first sentence, "The light in the mind destroys the moving object." He read the second—"When doubt arises among the trees, nothing is hidden." He read the first two sentences again, then realized they were words he had written two weeks ago. He picked up the notebook and held it open at arms length. It was his paragraph! He wrote it the last time he used his green pen two weeks before. He looked again. The third sentence made him stop writing for the day and close the notebook. It read, "This happiness arrives in the silence of a mistake."

TO TELL

I would like the stillness to be what it has to be, its steady curtain delaying the start of the game. I would like to have descended through a passage of absence that doesn't allow fear or escape, been there for the embrace, a move toward placing my hands upon the needy abstraction that keeps my breath at bay. I would like to be able to see it, at last, and describe its immense involvement, a fusion of a real thing with what should have stepped before me despite the dimension of questions that got in the way.

I would like to spell the form and the color, involve the hair on the glass and the dust in the eye that blinks toward oblivion without faith, convincing me not to move from this spot because there are preoccupied things coming my way. I would like to name the moments like notebooks stripped of bark and identifiable growth, pages where the story ends before it begins, a passage recalling how I entered the heart and came out somewhere through the brain.

I would like to admire the sentence I erased, how the blur of letters remains on this page, thoughts catching up with what was there before I rearranged the future to pass through unbearable light that grayed my head, hid what I actually meant before it revealed the table where I sat down and ate, fulfilling the world whose madness is measured through the blue cup on the table when I rose and fled, my consequences propelling me to compose a habit whose thousand hours of silence resemble a man sitting down, this time unharmed, wondering what made him so afraid.

ACKNOWLEDGMENTS

I thank the editors of the following publications in which these poems first appeared:

Bitter Oleander: "I Can't Help Myself," "My Stone, My Mask," "The Last Mayan Indian" and "The Small Searchlight";

Bombay Gin: "I Smell";

Cerise Press Journal: "Erase the Seventh Moon," "James Wright Returns to Minneapolis," "Retrieval," "Six Rising Prose Poems," and "The Same Window";

Colorado Review: "Beginning with Two Lines from Kenneth Rexroth," and "Distrust Creation";

Fifth Wednesday: "Canto" and "The Sky is Beautiful";

Hayden's Ferry Review: "To Tell";

Hotel Amerika: "Available for an Epiphany," "The Cross," and "21st Century Friend";

Practice: "Alternative Similarity";

Quarter After Eight: "Ten Objects";

Sentence: "Findings (1)" and "The Guitars";

Tammy: "Dada Means Elephant";

TriQuarterly: "Findings (2)" and "Findings (3)."

"The Guitars" appeared in *The Rose Metal Press Field Guide to Prose Poetry: Contemporary Poets in Discussion and Practice* (Rose Metal Press, 2010).

The following poems appeared in *The Same Window,* a limited edition chapbook published by Mesilla Press, Minneapolis, Minnesota (2008): "Dada Means Elephant," "Erase the Seventh Moon," "Hit the Floor," "James Wright Returns to Minneapolis," "Jimi is Walking," "Let Me Disappear," "Pablo Picasso Spit in My Face," "Profit from Reality," "Set the Controls for the Heart of the Sun," "The Floating House," "The Same

Window," "Things You Don't See Anymore," "Wandering Packs of Gods," and "You Got the Spider".

I thank Peter Conners and Thom Ward for their support of my work over the years and acknowledge the influence of fellow poets and friends who work in the prose poem—George Kalamaras, John Bradley, Morton Marcus, and Peter Johnson. I thank the University of Minnesota's Scholar of the College Award for fellowship support that gave me time to write these poems.

ABOUT THE AUTHOR

Ray Gonzalez is the author of eleven books of poetry, including five from BOA Editions: *The Heat of Arrivals* (1997 PEN/Oakland Josephine Miles Book Award), *Cabato Sentora* (2000 Minnesota Book Award Finalist), *The Hawk Temple at Tierra Grande* (winner of a 2003 Minnesota Book Award for Poetry) and *Consideration of the Guitar: New and Selected Poems* (2005) and *Cool Auditor (2009). Turtle Pictures* (Arizona, 2000), a mixed-genre text, received the 2001 Minnesota Book Award for Poetry. His poetry has appeared in the 1999, 2000, and 2003 editions of *The Best American Poetry* (Scribners) and *The Pushcart Prize: Best of the Small Presses 2000* (Pushcart Press). He is also the author of three collections of essays, *The Underground Heart: A Return to a Hidden Landscape* (Arizona, 2002), which received the 2003 Carr P. Collins/ Texas Institute of Letters Award for Best Book of Non-fiction, *Memory Fever* (University of Arizona Press, 1999), a memoir about growing up in the Southwest, and *Renaming the Earth: Personal Essays* (Arizona, 2008). He has written two collections of short stories, *The Ghost of John Wayne* (Arizona, 2001, winner of a 2002 Western Heritage Award for Best Short Story and a 2002 Latino Heritage Award in Literature) and *Circling the Tortilla Dragon* (Creative Arts, 2002). He is the editor of twelve anthologies, most recently *Sudden Fiction Latino* (co-edited with Robert Shapard and James Thomas, W.W. Norton, 2010) and *No Boundaries: Prose Poems by 24 American Poets* (Tupelo Press, 2002). He has served as Poetry Editor of The Bloomsbury Review for twenty-five years and founded LUNA, a poetry journal, in 1998. He is Full Professor in the MFA Creative Writing Program at The University of Minnesota in Minneapolis and also teaches in the Solstice low residency MFA Program at Pine Manor College in Boston.

BOA Editions, Ltd.
American Poets Continuum Series

COLOPHON

Cool Auditor, by Ray Gonzalez is set in Lucida Bright, designed by Charles Bigelow and Kris Holmes in 1985. The headlines are set in Trajan Pro designed in 1989 by Carol Twombly for Adobe. The design is based on the letterforms of capitalis monumentalis or Roman square capitals, as used for the inscription at the base of Trajan's Column from which the typeface takes its name.

The publication of this book is made possible, in part, by the following individuals:

Anonymous

Alan & Nancy Cameros

Rome Celli & Elizabeth Forbes

Gwen & Gary Conners

Wyn Cooper & Shawna Parker

Peter & Suzanne Durant

Pete & Bev French

Judy & Dane Gordon

Kip & Debby Hale

Bob & Willy Hursh

Robin Hursh

Nora A. Jones

X. J. & Dorothy M. Kennedy

Dorianne Laux & Joseph Millar

Rosemary & Lewis Lloyd

Donna M. Marbach

Boo Poulin, in honor of Susan Burke & Bill Leonardi

Deborah Ronnen & Sherman Levey

Paul & Andrea Rubery

Steven O. Russell & Phyllis Rifkin-Russell

Vicki & Richard Schwartz

Joel & Friederike Seligman

Pat & Mike Wilder

Glenn & Helen William